Caroline Alexander was a Rhodes Scholar at Oxford reading Philosophy and Theology. She received her doctorate in Classics in 1991 from Columbia University, New York. In 1982-5 she established a small Classics department at the University of Malawi. She now lives on a farm in New Hampshire and is a regular contributor to the *New Yorker*.

The Way to Xanadu

CAROLINE ALEXANDER

PHŒNIX

Map of East Florida and the River St John taken from *Travels in North and South
Carolina, Georgia, East and West Florida and the Cherokee Country* by William Bartram
(Philadelphia 1791) reproduced by courtesy of the British Library.

Map of North and Eastern Africa: Drawn in the 1400's showing Ptolemy's Mountain
of the Moon as the Source of the River Nile, Hart 7195 82v-83 Harley Manuscripts,
British Library, London/Bridgeman Art Library, London.

Map of Kashmir taken from *Travels in the Mogul Empire*. AD 1656-1668, translated
by Irving Brock, edited by Archibald Constable (London 1914).

Two maps of Shangtu appear courtesy of *The Geographical Review*, a publication
of the American Geographical Society (Vol 15, 1925).

To George,
who let me lead the way.

ACKNOWLEDGEMENTS

I owe many debts to many people for this
book. In addition to those named in the text, I
would like to thank the following; Professor
C. T. Hsia, my mother Elizabeth Kirby, Dr
Richard Lynn, Jan Mitchell, William Rayner
and Dr Morris Rossabi.
Special debts of gratitude are owed
– as always – to Laura Slatkin;
and to Robert Gottlieb,
who sent me on the way.

Contents

Faust: *Wohin der Weg?*
Mephistopheles: *Kein Weg!*'

Kubla Khan

or a vision in a dream. A fragment.

In Xanadu did Kubla Khan
A stately pleasure-dome decree:
Where Alph, the sacred river, ran
Through caverns measureless to man
    Down to a sunless sea.
So twice five miles of fertile ground
With walls and towers were girdled round:
And there were gardens bright with sinuous rills,
Where blossomed many an incense-bearing tree;
And here were forests ancient as the hills,
Enfolding sunny spots of greenery.

But oh! that deep romantic chasm which slanted
Down the green hill athwart a cedarn cover!
A savage place! as holy and enchanted
As e'er beneath a waning moon was haunted
By woman wailing for her demon-lover!
And from this chasm, with ceaseless turmoil seething,
As if this earth in fast thick pants were breathing,
A mighty fountain momently was forced:
Amid whose swift half-intermitted burst
Huge fragments vaulted like rebounding hail,
Or chaffy grain beneath the thresher's flail:
And 'mid these dancing rocks at once and ever
It flung up momently the sacred river.

Five miles meandering with a mazy motion
Through wood and dale the sacred river ran,
Then reached the caverns measureless to man,
And sank in tumult to a lifeless ocean:
And 'mid this tumult Kubla heard from far
Ancestral voices prophesying war!
 The shadow of the dome of pleasure
 Floated midway on the waves;
 Where was heard the mingled measure
 From the fountain and the caves.
It was a miracle of rare device,
A sunny pleasure-dome with caves of ice!

 A damsel with a dulcimer
 In a vision once I saw:
 It was an Abyssinian maid,
 And on her dulcimer she played,
 Singing of Mount Abora.
 Could I revive within me
 Her symphony and song,
 To such a deep delight 'twould win me,
That with music loud and long,
I would build that dome in air,
That sunny dome! those caves of ice!
And all who heard should see them there,
And all should cry, Beware! Beware!
His flashing eyes, his floating hair!
Weave a circle round him thrice,
And close your eyes with holy dread,
For he on honey-dew hath fed,
And drunk the milk of Paradise.

Preface

Like many people, I first encountered Samuel Taylor Coleridge's masterpiece 'Kubla Khan' while of school age, reading it without full comprehension, but with a visceral conviction of its greatness. It has been said of the poem that as with dreams and visions, one asks, 'what do you think it means?' It has never seemed to me that 'Kubla Khan' is *about* anything. There is no overt action, for example, only shifting scenes and a hint of events to come ('And 'mid this tumult Kubla heard from far / Ancestral voices prophesying war!'). Like Yahweh in Genesis, the great Khan effects events by will or decree, himself remaining an awe-ful shadow presence behind the scenes, omnipotent in capability, but at the moment passive.

None the less, the poem resonates with possibilities, all of which pertain to humanity's most basic drives – power, wealth, sex, death, and the desire to create enduring objects of beauty. These primal compulsions are not evoked by a human actor or agent; the poem does not describe Kubla Khan, or any other person – it describes land.

With the exception of the poem's final stanza, virtually every line is descriptive of landscape – and landscape that, although exotic, is not fanciful. The realm of Xanadu may strike one as being a hopelessly romantic fabrication, but its individual features are not altogether unfamiliar – walled gardens and forests, scented trees, rivers and chasms and spectacular displays of water – we have all seen some of these. 'Kubla Khan's' great strength, it seemed to me, was that it could transport one to a realm of the imagination by means of images that were altogether of this world; and in so doing, it offered the reminder that the natural world of experience could be similarly transporting.

The circumstances of 'Kubla Khan's' creation have led many scholars to regard it as the supreme example of purely imaginative composition. Coleridge's own account of the manner in which this happened is almost as famous as the poem itself, and more often than not is published with it as a preface:

> In the summer of 1797, the Author, then in ill health, had retired to a lonely farm-house between Porlock and Linton, on the Exmoor confines of Somerset and Devonshire. In consequence of a slight indisposition, an anodyne had been prescribed, from the effects of which he fell asleep in his chair at the moment that he was reading the following sentence, or words of the same substance, in 'Purchas's Pilgrimage': 'Here the Khan Kubla commanded a palace to be built, and a stately garden thereunto. And thus ten miles of fertile ground were inclosed with a wall.'

According to Coleridge, the poem was composed in the profound opium sleep that followed; 'if that indeed can be called composition in which all the images rose up before him as *things* ...' On awakening, he began at once to recall the dream-poem on paper, finishing some fifty-five lines before he 'was unfortunately called out by a person on business from Porlock'. This visit lasted an hour, and when Coleridge finally freed himself to return to his poem, he found it beyond recollection: '... with the exception of some eight or ten scattered lines and images, all the rest had passed away like the images on the surface of a stream into which a stone has been cast ...'

Supreme of the images that did remain was that of Xanadu, whose dream origins and romantic imagery for a long while led me to assume that it was fictive. But eventually my long fascination with the poem goaded me into undertaking some research on its Mongol namesake; and I discovered that although not appearing on any modern atlas, Xanadu, or Shangdu as it is more properly called, was 'real', and lay in what is now the Zhenglan Banner of the Autonomous Republic of Inner Mongolia, in northeast China. Although I knew that I would not be travelling through the exotic landscape of Coleridge's vision, still, the unexpected possibility of crossing the physical threshold of this legendary site was not to be resisted. Whatever I might find, a trip to Xanadu would be, I believed, the single most romantic journey of a lifetime.

THE
WALLS
AND
TOWERS

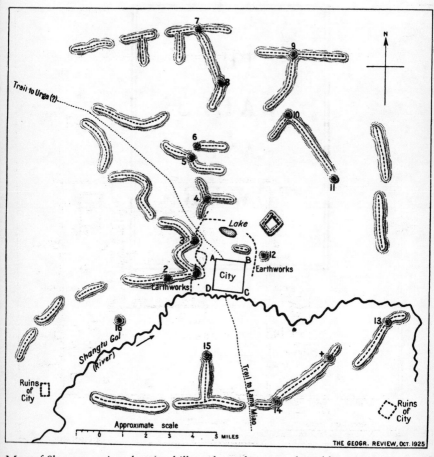

Map of Shangtu region showing hills and watchtowers plotted by compass bearings, rivers sketched in approximately. (The numbers on the map refer to compass bearings which appear in the original caption in the *Geographical Review*, 1925).

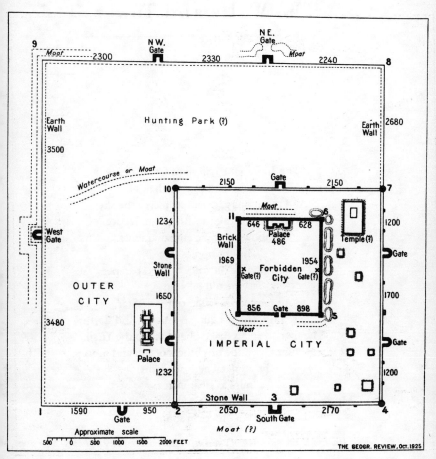

Reprinted with the permission of The American Geographical Society from *Geographical Review*, 1925.

The Walls and Towers

The Imperial Pavilion of Great Peace
thrusts upward to great heights,
And gorgeous gate towers pierce the sky
endowing Shangdu with magnificence.
Rainbows encircle embankments,
bright ripples fine;
Dragons writhe on whitewashed parapets,
emerald hills flat.
All luminaries salute our Pole Star,
for here is greatness equal to Heaven and Earth;
The myriad states make obeisance to the Yuan,
for It shines with the brightness of sun and moon.
From detached jade halls,
pure as clear water,
Music of the ancient Sage-King Shun is sometime heard –
phoenixes in song.

Jia Lu, Commander of the Imperial Forces (1297–1353)

These gate towers of Heaven reach into the great void,
Yet city walls are low enough to welcome distant hills.

Miscellaneous Songs on the Upper Capital

My inspired journey was almost blocked at the outset by the prosaic fact that the remains of Xanadu, or Shangdu, in northeast China, lie in an 'army occupied area' closed to foreigners. In the autumn of 1988, however, the year in which I first determined to attempt the trip, I received a telephone call from an old friend, who was attending university in the western United States. In answer to her question about what I was then planning to do with my life, I replied, with an edge of smugness, that I was contemplating a trip to Xanadu, if I could find a way round the daunting Chinese bureaucracy.

'I am getting a degree in Mongolian and Central Asian archae-ology,' replied Stella, annoyingly unsurprised, and offered to provide me with a bibliography of works that I should read before setting out.

'In fact,' she said, 'my major professor is an expert on this subject. I can send you some of his articles. His name is Dr John Olsen.'

My memory stirred: had Dr Olsen once lived in Florida, I asked? Stella replied that she thought he had. As we spoke, I was standing in the kitchen of my mother's home in Tallahassee, in north Florida, looking out of the window at the white house across the road that I used to visit almost daily as a child, when I had played with my friend John Olsen. He had been my first playmate when my family had moved to the USA. I had not seen or heard of him since I was twelve years old.

'Well,' said the voice lazily at the other end of the line, when I called the number Stella had given me. 'This goes back some years.' As my luck would have it, he could claim the friendship of a high ranking official in The Bureau of Cultural Relics in Inner Mongolia, and he promised to see what he could do. The Tiananmen Square uprising, however, erupted some months later, and all plans of going to China had to be postponed. But when, two years later, I was ready to try again, Dr Olsen happened to be posted for the year in Beijing, and was thus able to act as a direct liaison between me and the Inner Mongolian authorities.

Months of silence passed, broken only by an occasional letter or fax from John, relaying or requesting information. I had resigned myself to a long period of indefinite resolution when one morning in June, I awoke to find what appeared to be an ancient Chinese scroll unfurled across the floor. It was a lengthy fax, handwritten in Chinese characters, that had come in overnight from the authorities in Hoh-hot, the capital of Inner Mongolia. It contained an itinerary, an estimate of expenses, and, surmounted by a facsimile seal, a visa issued for myself and my travelling companion, George, to visit Shangdu.

Khubilai Khan was, of course, not the only Mongolian Khaghan, or Great Khan, nor was Shangdu his only imperial residence. Khubilai was born on 23 September 1215, the fourth of four brothers, and a grandson of Genghis Khan, the legendary warlord whose unified nomadic forces extended Mongol power from China to the Adriatic and made his name a byword for terror. His father Tolui, the young-est of Genghis's sons by his favourite wife, had been a military man, whose heavy drinking had probably led to his death at the age of forty-two. His mother, Sorghaghtani Beki, was recognised as being one of the most remarkable women of her age, and her intelligence, administrative abilities and upbringing of her sons were widely praised by contemporary writers. She was a Nestorian Christian, but notably tolerant of other religions, a trait that was also to characterise her son. Khubilai was brought up in the Mongol homelands, the share of Genghis's empire that had been allocated to Tolui along with Northern China shortly after his father's death: the Genghisid line of power had passed to Tolui and his descendants as the result of a *coup d'état* in 1250, made at the cost of Ögödei, Genghis's chosen successor and Tolui's brother – disputes over the legitimacy of claims to the throne were to continue throughout Khubilai's reign, and past his death.

A contemporary portrait of Khubilai by the Chinese artist Liu Guandao shows a smooth, round-faced man with dark hair and beard, heavy jowls and shrewd eyes, possessed of an expression of great complacency: its accuracy, however, must be questioned, given its striking similarity to a portrait of Genghis Khan dating from the same era, save that the generic face has in this case been given wispy white hair and whiskers. According to the thirteenth-century Persian historian Rashīd al-Dīn, Khubilai was 'swarthy'; Marco Polo, on the other hand, describes him as being 'fair and ruddy like a rose'.

The Great Khan, he notes, was of moderate height, with 'black hand-some eyes' and a shapely nose 'set squarely in place', evidently a noteworthy trait amidst his subject Chinese population.

In 1251, at the age of thirty-six, Khubilai was mandated civil and military authority over Mongolian China by his ruling brother, Möngke, a turn of affairs that brought him into the political limelight. Like other Mongol leaders before him, Möngke was intent upon the subjugation of China, an undertaking in which Khubilai played a decisive part by leading significant victories in the territory of the southern Sung kingdom. This campaign was brought to a temporary and inconclusive end, however, with the death of Möngke in 1259, when Khubilai's attention was subsequently turned to the more personally pressing issue of succession. Word had come to him that his youngest brother, Ariqböke, who had been left to administer the Mongol homelands, was making a bid for their brother's title.

The two brothers were of very different views regarding the future orientation of the contested empire, with Ariqböke seeking to sustain the primacy of traditional nomadic steppe life, and Khubilai drawn towards the sedentary life, particularly as manifested by the Chinese imperial court. This dispute with his brother was not to end definitively until Ariqböke's death (reportedly of natural causes) some years later. None the less on 5 May 1260, at his residence Shangdu, Khubilai was unanimously elected as the sixth Great Khan at a hastily gathered *khuriltai*, or Mongol princely assembly. His throne secured, Khubilai resumed his campaign in southern China, and the eventual dismantling of the Sung dynasty in 1279 marked the conclusive subjugation of China as a whole. It was the first time since the Tang dynasty, which had ended in the early tenth century, that China had been united.

At the time of Khubilai's reign, the empire of the Yuan dynasty – the Mongol dynasty founded in 1206 through brute military force by Genghis Khan, though, properly, only named in 1271 by Khubilai – extended from the Qipchaq steppe and Persian Gulf to the Indus river and the East China Sea. As Great Khan, Khubilai was not only ruler of China, but the supreme lord of all the individual Mongol domains, including the Persian *Il–khanate*, the Golden Horde of southern Russia and the Mongolian steppes; his subjects represented the largest population thus far in history to acknowledge the sovereignty of a single man. Recognising that the traditional political framework of the Mongols, who were, after all, a nomadic people, was not remotely equipped to govern an empire, Khubilai surrounded himself with a staff of Confucian advisers and relied upon the anciently established bureaucracy that he had inherited from the Chinese, along with their empire, although for reasons of security he made a practice of staffing it with foreigners (such as the Venetian merchant Marco Polo).

Khubilai's reign was characterised by clemency towards his foes in war, and tolerance in times of peace towards his subjects, who were allowed to continue the practice of their traditional religions, customs and arts unmolested. All evidence indicates that the Great Khan was a man possessed of an enormous worldly appetite and unbounded curiosity, and a considerable amount of his energy seems to have been devoted to the encouragement of those enterprises that could garner him knowledge about the world beyond his vast domain. To this end, expeditions were mounted that ventured as far as Madagascar and Java, while special privileges conferred upon merchants ensured a far-reaching exchange of commodities and ideas – the extensive trade routes encompassed within his empire, it has been claimed, provided foreign trade and intercourse not matched until modern times.

Although the Mongolians, as nomads, had traditionally been tent-dwellers, an imperial residence had been established as early as Genghis Khan's rule. Karakorum, away in the heart of the steppes, had been a wall-enclosed complex consisting of a military garrison and markets. Initially it had been comprised of tents, but under Ghengis's successors permanent structures were introduced. Similarly, although the keeping of different seasonal residences had been practised by at least one Mongol khan before Khubilai, it is none the less he who is remembered for being the greatest builder of his dynasty. Khubilai was eventually to establish four palace cities, which were visited in turn according to the season. Of these, the two earliest would remain the most important: Shangdu ('Upper Capital', also referred to as Chandu, Sandu, Luanjing, Shangji, Keminfu and Kaiping), his official summer residence, and the Yuan capital proper, Dadu, the site of modern-day Beijing.

Khubilai shrewdly took great pains to ensure that he be viewed as a legitimate Chinese emperor, rather than a conquering barbarian Mongol, and architecturally as well as bureaucratically his court had a distinctively Chinese cast. For all this, he was never completely absorbed by the culture of his conquered people, and Yuan historians record that he gave orders for the fragrant steppe grass to be brought to his palace in Dadu, so that his descendants might not be forgetful of the land in which they had originated, nor he himself of his humble origins. In the same vein, Shangdu served not only as a retreat from the lowland heat, but as a place where the Khan could practise the hunting and riding arts of his people and relax in Mongolian style.

> Out the Pass, travelling with face raised to the sun,
> Hurrying to Court, delighted to be approaching Heaven –
> Where the Detached Palace opens to its pleasure gardens,
> The Royal Thoroughfare stays free of wind and mist.

Liu Guan

The fourth moon of every year marked the departure of the Great Khan and his retinue from Dadu to his summer residence. Before he left, Khubilai held a feast for his officials in the *Lingyu*, or Zoological Gardens, which lay to the east of the Hill of Ten Thousand Years. As the Great Khan left his island palace in its artificial lake, the *liushouguan*, or 'officer who stays behind to guard', cut the bridges, to prohibit passage until he should return.

According to Marco Polo, the retinue accompanying Khubilai on a hunting expedition from Dadu included as many as ten thousand falconers. The Great Khan himself

> always rides on the back of four elephants, in a very handsome shelter of wood, covered inside with cloth of beaten gold and outside with lion skins. Here he always keeps twelve gerfalcons of the best he possesses and is attended by several barons to

entertain him and keep him company. When he is travelling in this shelter on the elephants, and other barons who are riding in his train call out, 'Sire, there are cranes passing,' and he orders the roof of the shelter to be thrown open and so sees the cranes, he bids his attendants fetch such gerfalcons as he may choose and lets them fly. And often, the gerfalcons take the cranes in full view while the Great Khan remains all the while on his couch. And this affords him great sport and recreation.

The Great Khan remained at Shangdu throughout the summer months, ending his sojourn on the same day of every year, the twenty-eighth of August. The elaborate ceremony of departure for the return trip to Dadu, as described by Marco Polo, betrayed a specifically Mongolian character: mare's milk, from the Khan's stable of over ten thousand snow-white mares and stallions, was flung into the air and poured on the earth as a libation offering to the spirits that guarded the Khan's possessions, his 'men and women, beasts, birds, crops, and everything besides'.

Shangdu lay at a distance of fifty parasangs from the Great Court, or about one hundred and sixty-two miles due north, a journey of approximately ten days for the cumbersome procession. The rate of travel was leisurely, and frequent stops were held for hawking. Along the route at intervals of three to four miles, stood watchtowers and post houses equipped with runners, providing military protection, convenient halting places and communications centres. According to Marco Polo, the postal system was so efficient that within ten days news could be transmitted over the distance of a journey of a hundred days. He adds that in the fruit season, produce gathered in the morning in Dadu could be delivered by evening of the next day at Shangdu.

The specific route taken by Khubilai on this seasonal migration is decribed in some detail by Rashīd al-Dīn:

There are three roads from the winter residence: one road which is reserved for hunting and along which no one may travel except couriers; another road by way of Joju [modern Joxian], to which one travels along the banks of the River Sangin, where there is [an] abundance of grapes and other fruit and near which is another small town called Sinali, the people of which are mostly from Samarqand and have laid out gardens in the Samarqand fashion; and there is another road, by way of a low hill, which they call Sing-Ling, and when one passes over that hill the steppe is all grassland and [suitable for] summer pasturage up to the town of Kemin-Fu [that is, Shangdu].

Theoretically, as the crow flies, one could today reach the ruins of Shangdu after no more than one day's travel from modern Beijing. No simple, direct road, however, exists from one place to the other, although a Chinese traveller may make the journey in a roundabout way by local buses. The official itinerary laid out for George and me described a tortuously triangular route: first, we were to fly from Beijing to Hohhot, the capital of the Inner Mongolian Autonomous Region, some two hundred miles to the northwest of Beijing; then from Hohhot to Xilinhot some three hundred miles to the northeast; thence, an indeterminate distance to a village to the south, from where at last we would be in striking distance of the ruins of Xanadu.

Nei Menggu, or Inner Mongolia, is one of five autonomous regions of the People's Republic of China. At an average elevation of approximately three thousand feet, it is essentially an upland plateau ringed by mountains, which in the northwest slopes away towards the Gobi Desert. It encompasses an area of nearly 164,000 square miles, with an eight-hundred-mile borderline with northern China. To the west, south and east it is bounded by other Chinese provinces, and to the north by the Mongolian People's Republic, or Outer Mongolia.

The distinction between Inner and Outer Mongolia was made as early as the seventeenth century, although in modern times it has tended to be taken as indicating the territories' alliances with the People's Republic of China and, until recently, the Soviet Union. The Mongol population has been reduced even in relatively recent years by disease: in the last century bubonic plague was endemic, and as late as the late 1940s an estimated sixty per cent of the adult population was inflicted with syphilis. In Chinese Mongolia, immigrant Han Chinese now outnumber Mongolians by a ratio of over eight to one; as much as eighty-four per cent of the region's total population of nearly twenty million is Chinese, while only ten per cent is Mongol, with various minority groups – including Manchus, Koreans, Dahurs and Ewenkis – accounting for the remaining odd six per cent.

The historically well-established mix of Chinese agrarian and Mongolian pastoral cultures is retained today, although the extreme harshness of the winter prohibits extensive agricultural exploitation of this rich land. The majority of the population are found just north of the Chinese–Nei Menggu border, indicating, as it were, the high-water mark of the incoming, and ongoing, flow of Chinese immigrants. A map of Inner Mongolia typically shows a vast brown expanse, indicating its miles upon miles of windy grassland, scratched by a few tenuous red lines that demarcate roads. The further north one goes, away from the settlements and handful of really big cities, the more in touch one can believe oneself to be with the 'real' Mongolia, the steppeland of herdsmen and horsemen. This view falters when comparison is made with Outer Mongolia, however, whose population of just two million luxuriates in an area of undeveloped grasslands well over three times the size of Nei Menggu.

Hohhot (a less merciful spelling is Huhehaote) was established as the region's capital in 1954. The perpetual briskness of the air that blows in from the steppes, together with the city's slight elevation, give its atmosphere a chilling, blue-tinged clarity: even bright sunlight appears wan and cold, and the town's monumental Soviet-style architecture – broad, barren thoroughfares and the calculated space of its 'people's squares' – seems to have been etched against a panoramic backdrop of rarefied space. This physical and spiritual coldness is mitigated here and there by odd touches of colour, such as the surprising number of flowers in pots and shade trees that edge the roads, or the whimsical events staged in the People's Park – a predawn foxtrotting dance club, for example, or dromedary rides. Temples and vestiges of the old town, which dates from the sixteenth century, can be found in the jumbled streets that lie safe miles from the highrise concrete of the 'new city'.

The resurgent nationalism that has marked the recent history of the Mongolian Republic has no parallel in Chinese Mongolia. The potentially dangerous cult of Genghis Khan that has resurfaced in Outer Mongolia to great political effect has been cannily pre-empted by the Chinese authorities controlling Nei Menggu: one of the two most visible icons, represented in plaster statuary and a variety of logo-style paintings, is of the proud Mongolian warlord, usually rendered with ambiguous Eurasian features. Appearing blatantly everywhere as he does, the subliminal message appears to be that, there being manifestly nothing subversive in replicating his image, he must be a kind of Chinese hero. (The other icon, incidentally, is the cheerful panda that is assiduously marketed as the embodiment of New China, and which is increasingly coming to resemble Mickey Mouse.)

Further evidence of the official Chinese attitude to things Mongolian is to be found in the Museum of Inner Mongolia, which houses both Chinese and Mongolian artefacts, such as Mongolian saddles and traditional costumes. The term – 'cultural relics' – used to describe these objects struck me as being an unwarrantedly cynical label for a culture that, albeit much diminished, is not yet quite extinct. Although the official reason for the site of Xanadu being off-limits to foreigners is that it trespasses on militarily sensitive territory, it is also possible that the Chinese government does not relish the prospect of a trail of tourism coming to pay homage to the former imperial residence of the Great Khan – and only foreigner – who held the whole of China in his thrall.

Under the terms of the visas issued to George and me, our exploration of the site had to be made in the close and abiding company of a handful of officials. Luckily for us, the extreme good nature of the chosen individuals meant that this was to be no hardship. The representative from the Bureau of Cultural Relics, who oversaw our welcome, was a handsome Mongolian man whom I judged to be in his late forties, possessed of the kind of inscrutable dignity with which Hollywood fondly endows its Red Indians and other Noble Savages: impassive, chiselled features, bolt-upright bearing. When he addressed us, he looked somewhere into middle distance above our heads, where he would hold his gaze while his utterance was translated – indeed, his whole manner was that of a man accustomed to having his words translated to peons.

The interpreter chosen to accompany us throughout the journey was a young Chinese woman named Na. Her delicate features wore a perpetual soft frown of concentration and mild anxiety, which I took to be the direct result of her commission to come between us and the Chinese world over the next week or so. She had a certain instinctive flair that led one to believe that she had seen something of the world, yet for all her quiet style, she had in fact ventured only once or twice outside Hohhot, the city of her birth. She was a student of English literature, however, and I surmised that it was this that accounted in part for her distinctive, outward-looking air.

Mr Hada was the representative from the Bureau chosen to oversee our excursion. Unlike Na, the burden of his assignment appeared to rest very lightly on his shoulders. His face was either creased in a grin or crumpled in a toothy smile. He was a young and energetic man, his movements characteristically restless and abrupt. Unmistakably, the opportunity of our upcoming trip was personally welcome to him, and he intended to enjoy its every minute.

A few words should also be added to introduce George, who is in essence a man who would undoubtedly have been happiest living as a gentleman in nineteenth-century England. Like his British forebears, he possesses a clear, binding and utterly obsolete code of personal honour, which he naïvely believes to bind his contemporary fellow men, a blind spot that has led to many a pitfall. He is also a genuine outdoorsman and, more unusually, the producer and director of the movie *Pumping Iron*, and so responsible in great part for bringing Arnold Schwarzenegger to the world's attention.

The morning flight to Xilinhot was made in a tiny prop plane that lurched into a sky of harsh, pristine blue. Below us, the green swathes of Hohhot's parks and gardens became suddenly lost to a dull brown wash of sand and sediment, cut by ox-blood-coloured rivulets and dried-up streams. A scalloped line indicated the terraced foothills of the Daqing Mountains, which appeared as a bank of dramatic contours. Like a last sighting of land before setting out to sea, this range represented the last identifiable feature on the earth before we launched over the mustard-coloured barrenness that is Mongolia.

One and a half hours later, the plane touched down on a field of bumpy turf. In front of the single airport building a small crowd was already jostling in readiness to surge forward and claim places on the plane on its turnaround flight back to Hohhot. Towering conspicuously above all the other people was a tall, angular, shaven-headed figure – and the only other European we were to meet in Nei Menggu – who called out to us urgently as we passed.

'Book your flight back immediately! There are only two flights out a week. Book your flight back now!'

The fact that one arrives at Xilinhot not by way of a progression of other towns, cities or villages, but after a flight over a desolate stretch of barren grasslands indicates that Xilinhot did not arise 'naturally' in the vanguard of ordinary waves of settlement, but was calculatedly placed upon this spot. A booklet that I came across representing an optimistic stab at a nascent tourist industry proclaims Xilinhot 'the Shining Pearl on the Grassland', but in the next breath adds the prosaic fact that the city is in 'an area with rich underground minerals'. Xilinhot is, in many respects, a last frontier; it is the most remote point to which foreigners are normally allowed to travel, and for this reason is the best place from which to see the grasslands and remnants of Mongolian traditional life – for the present, at least, for in Xilinhot the future of Inner Mongolia as envisaged by the controlling Chinese authorities is unambiguously revealed. For all its one hundred thousand inhabitants, Xilinhot is merely a frontier town, built in preparation for the carefully projected boom that will follow the mass exploitation of the 'rich underground minerals', lovingly enumerated in the tourist booklet as 'reserves of chromium, copper, iron, tin, as well as natural alkali, mirabilite, marble, refractory clay and limestone', in addition to the large reserves of oil and coal on the city outskirts.

The town itself is purposefully laid out on a no-nonsense grid of wide, functional streets and unadorned buildings. The brand-new residential houses are attractive in their way, somewhat resembling solid, brick cottages and, en masse, reminiscent of a Victorian housing estate. Each is contained by a surrounding wall, which we were told is the custom of the country – perhaps for privacy, perhaps as an extra buffer between the winds and snows of Mongolian winter. While the average temperature in summer is around seventy-seven degrees Fahrenheit, on bitter winter nights the icy winds from Siberia bring it down to as much as forty degrees below zero. A mild wind blew continuously at the time of our visit, with an occasional biting gust by way of warning that it is a factor that must always be taken seriously. Indeed, the city looks wind-scoured, as if a great dust storm had just rolled through it.

Because we were officially under the auspices of the Bureau of Cultural Relics, it had been deemed necessary that we visit Shangdu not only under escort of the Hohhot delegation, but in the presence of the Director of Xilinhot's Cultural Relics Station. Mr Batu was a Mongolian of untypically lanky build and height. His face beneath luxuriant salt-and-pepper greyed hair was the colour of copper, and his narrow eyes seemed to squint at the sun from behind his heavy glasses, a tendency that was exaggerated by his habit of turning his face up towards the sky. He was the most smartly dressed individual I encountered in the whole of China, and on meeting us was wearing a trilby hat, a dark checked suit and a tie pinned neatly by a minuscule portrait of Genghis Khan. Having seen us safely settled into the local hotel, he announced that he would take us to the grasslands. 'Grasslands' was a word that I had heard reverently whispered since our arrival in China: 'You will see the grasslands.' 'You are going up north? Then you must see the grasslands.'

'I am looking forward very much to seeing the grasslands,' Na had said to me in Hohhot, and it was from her demurely contained excitement that I glimpsed how far away this legendary realm was to the average Chinese person.

Turning out of Xilinhot, a single narrow road curved into low hills and the grasslands proper, a mustardy-gold plain of tufted grass. The annual rains of July and August briefly transform this prairie into an unbounded meadow of succulent tender green; but we were at summer's end, and apart from scanty showers, the rain had long since evaporated under the unrelenting sunshine of the perpetually windswept skies.

Some distance out, and we came upon an enormous domed tent erected on a wooden platform, which we were told was a reconstruction of Genghis Khan's palatial yurt, and a remnant of the set for a Chinese television film about his life. Although its imperial silks had been badly tattered by the wind and it wore an air of general neglect, the yurt was soon to be put to new use as the rallying point in an annual festival of traditional Mongol sports to be held a few months hence. A truck had been drawn up to one side of the platform, from which some workers were unloading an extraordinarily large supply of beer, which was to be laid down under the Great Khan's floorboards.

Small blips appearing against the mustard-coloured plain resolved themselves as we drew closer into a tiny settlement of three yurts, which resembled large steamed puddings bound in cheesecloth. A delicate tinker-toy windmill whirred incessantly beside them, firing the battery of a dented car parked beneath it next to a heavy, antiquated motorcycle. Beyond the yurts, three sturdy, shaggy ponies stood loosely tethered, one of them saddled and harnessed with an elaborate high-pommelled, silver-embossed saddle.

An old woman wearing a kerchief and the long caftan of Mongolian traditional dress came out of the kitchen and, after giving her welcome, invited us to step into one of the yurts. Inside, three Mongols, thoroughly modern and thoroughly drunk, greeted the lot of us – the Director, Na, Mr Hada, George and me – like brothers, and insisted that we join them in a drink.

'Traditional Mongolian hospitality,' whispered Na, who had clearly read all about this ethnic trait. A refined-looking woman sat discreetly to one side, both observer and participant in the ongoing, inescapable camaraderie. Many toasts of vodka were now drunk, interspersed with bowls of evil, salty tea and soft cheeses that tasted like *crème brûlée*. Eating and drinking seemed to be the principal activities of the yurtsmen, judging by the heaps of used cups and bowls and watermelon rinds that bedecked the hut. Milk products of one kind or another, and mutton, are the staples of Mongolian diet.

Other delicacies of the Xilinhot area show marked Chinese influence – hot candied camel hump, for example, or camel paws braised in brown sauce and bull's penis liquor.

Mongolian hospitality continued apace for some time, with the oldest of our hosts beginning to become aggressive in his refusal to accept my disinclination to drink more vodka.

'The Director is a typical Mongol,' whispered Na worriedly. And it was true that Mr Batu was manifestly loath to leave the springs of his native hospitality, and as we were all in his hands, we remained, like him, cross-legged in the yurt. The yurts themselves are essentially cosy domed tents of woollen felt stretched over a frame, which, as befits a nomadic people, is easily collapsible, and in this case was gaily painted red and blue. Brightly patterned rugs and cushions had been spread on the floor, and a low table placed in the middle of the room. A small shrine to Genghis Khan faced the entrance.

The sky had dimmed considerably by the time we were at last allowed to stumble outside. The little windmill was whirring more frenetically than ever, and a soft *whoosh* of wind passing through filled the barren space. In the distance, a herdsman was parading his long file of black and brown cattle. For the moment, livestock still ranks as Nei Menggu's primary economic activity, and Mongols therefore contribute significantly to the region's economy by practising their traditional way of life – as herdsmen and as tourist attractions. But in less than five years' time, Xilinhot is scheduled to have an international airport, with direct connections to Beijing, Ulaan Baatar, and points in what was formerly the Soviet Union. A tarmac runway is to be built on the grass strip on which our prop plane landed, and other reaches of the famous grasslands will, no doubt, be mined or under concrete. The Mongolians have been assiduously written into Chinese history up until this point, but it will be interesting to see how many of their traditional traits they will be encouraged to retain once this dream of industrial development is realised.

In the middle of the night before our departure to Shangdu, I awoke with the certainty that I was going to be ill in some as yet unspecified way, and sensed with sleepy indeterminacy that I was in a brief interlude between health and real trouble. In the morning I discovered that I did not want to leave my bed. For nearly two weeks beforehand, it was true, I had suffered from a racking cough that was the aftermath of a bad cold I picked up on travels George and I had made before coming to China. I felt this was now, suddenly, much worse, and I had moreover a dull pain in my lower back.

'We can stay, and leave tomorrow, Carolina,' said Na in her worried way, contemplating me while I still lay in bed.

'I think we should go as planned, and you can rest in the car; you will probably be better by the time we arrive at the site,' said George, ever the optimist. I agreed with him, as I was wary of the least change in schedule, and continually braced against an impending announcement that our special permits were no longer valid.

The Director, spruce and dapper in a new suit and jaunty hat, awaited us in the hotel driveway, where our official van had been parked. The weather had changed dramatically from the days before, and a windy rain lashed out upon us from dirty skies. All of Xilinhot's colour, I was now made to realise, had come from the sun, or had been a mere illusion of a blue heaven, and the reality abiding behind this bright veneer was a hard world of greyness and cold. The Director took his place in the front seat beside the driver who was, like him, Mongolian, and who had brought along his own supply of music – a single tape of 'Moscow Nights' sung in Chinese. George and Na took the row behind him, with Mr Hada in the jump seat beside them, and I went in the back. It had been my plan to sit up and quietly observe the land we were to pass through, and so be thoroughly rested and recovered by the time we actually drew close to Shangdu: but to my surprise, I found that I was unable to sit up at all and that it made me dizzy to look out of the window. The road ran before us, firm and undeviating, straight to the horizon, and yet for all the uncompromising confidence of its line seemed somehow senseless and random, as there was nothing, in whatever direction one might turn one's head, that could count as a 'destination' – not a hut, yurt, tree or hill marred the bleak contours of the grasslands.

'How are you feeling?' George asked every now and then, turning to where I lay stretched out on the back seat, and I replied, in all honesty, that I was all right. I did not feel ill, after all, just incapacitated. It was true that at certain moments I had begun to shake uncontrollably as if I were cold, but I had ascertained, by silent inward scrutiny, that this was the result of spasms of pain from my lower back. The fact that this was explicable made it seem reasonable, even in order.

From time to time over the next four hours I lifted my head to get a bearing, and in this disconnected way saw the grasslands give way to an expance of less wild turf; then to bleached dunes of sand sprouting little tufts of foliage; and then, as the day slowly brightened, again to a land of golden inviolate grass. The sky became once more irrevocably blue, studded with big, cheery mounds of clouds that cast massive swift-moving shadows. It did not seem to me that we were driving into a landscape of hills and mountains, valleys or geophysical features, but rather into rolling, ponderous shadows that in their constant moving continually recontoured the land. My head began to spin and I lay back down.

'Oh, you must see this!' George exclaimed somewhile later, looking out of the window, and I struggled up to see what had transfixed him. We seemed to have plunged into a scene from a Brueghel painting, or, alternatively, from a Chinese propaganda poster. The landscape that had showed few signs of a human presence, let alone habitation, for so many miles was now peopled by sturdy, bronzed, red-cheeked peasants dressed in blue Mao-style work uniforms industriously tending a blooming, fertile land. Harvesters wielded long, sweeping scythes and quick sickles; haywains, piled with golden grass, rocked and swayed behind the pulling oxen; haystacks stood like plump cairns in the gleaned fields – not a modern farming implement intruded on this almost medieval panorama. This scene of busy, improbably cheerful industry was permeated by an extraordinary golden light that seemed to shine out of the tawny fields. Only occasionally did one spot a pleasant brick-and-tile hamlet, and it was not evident from where this bustling populace had come.

In the early afternoon we came to a small town, where, the Director informed us, we would stop for a late lunch and rest. We drove into the rough courtyard of a guesthouse, which was built motel fashion, with its rooms forming one long wing. The thought of food of any kind nauseated me, and I was taken to one of the bedrooms – apparently, we were the only guests. It struck me, as I crossed the yard, that the town must be very new, so new that it did not yet sit comfortably under the sky, which seemed in its vastness to pour down upon it. The proprietor was a friendly Mongol woman, with hectic red cheeks and a long braid of black hair. My room was spartan, but I was appreciative of its modest virtues: its cleanliness, its restful, green and white walls, its well-boiled sheets, its quiet. Before she left for the dining room, Na looked in and outlined the remaining programme.

'We will rest here for a few hours. We will then drive to an historic site nearby, that is called Yenshan-tu, and is of the time that you are interested; then we will go to Duolun.'

Duolun was Dolonnur, the town which all travellers to Xanadu in the past had used as their point of reference: whenever I had written to the authorities in Hohhot about arranging a permit, I would describe Xanadu as 'Shangdu, the remains of Khubilai Khan's summer residence near Dolonnur'.

'And from Duolun we will go to Shangdu?' I now asked Na.

'Yes,' said Na, with her worried, gentle face looking down at me where I lay on the bed. 'It is not far from here, Carolina.'

A few hours later, we were back in the van. I had convinced myself that I felt better after the rest, and planned to sit up for this last, short leg of the trip; but as soon as we were on the road, I had second thoughts, and once again lay down.

A range of hills seemed to be rising ahead of us. The van veered to the left. The Director turned to shout something over 'Moscow Nights', which Na translated to mean that we were near the first site. I began to wish that we had postponed this mysterious 'historical site' for the return trip: I did not feel that I had energy for more than one place.

The van began to bump up and down, then turned right, and drew to a sudden halt. The doors were flung back, and the Director poked his head inside to say something. I started, feebly, to get out.

'If I were you, I'd stay inside,' said George, who had been looking for birds through his binoculars en route. 'If I see anything really interesting, I'll tell you.'

'We do not have to be long, Carolina,' said Na.

With relief, I lay back down. I had no curiosity about this particular site, what it was, whose it was, how it might relate to Khubilai Khan. Some forty-five minutes later, the group returned. George's face was beaming.

'It's pretty terrific there. I'd love to come back, if we get a chance. There's even loose pottery lying around.'

I had a brief vision of myself wandering over an overgrown ploughed field, slipping between old furrows and twisting my ankles in hidden rabbit-holes, and shuddered. Then, as the van got under way again, and recalling that we were now headed towards the place on earth I had planned and connived to get to for two years, I pulled myself together, and sat up. The day was glorious, the sky blue without flaw – blue without prettiness or vapidity, but profound and weighty, capable of filling the vast, otherwise unimpressionable land with sombre, heavy shadows. The dark range of hills towards which we were driving appeared to stretch across our path and block the way, but a cleft appeared between them, and through this the road could be seen spiralling up the peaty hills: it was the first stretch of road we had encountered so far that was not absolutely ruler-straight. I tried hard to take note of every detail, to commit the entire journey to memory – frowning hills; now cultivated fields; the outskirts of a bustling town, the roads made narrow by wayside fruit vendors and rolling, jostling wagons. Expecting that we would drive straight through the town, and continue on through countryside like that which lay behind us, I was startled when we pulled off the road into the compound of a large and vaguely officious-looking building. The driver turned off the engine.

Mr Batu, as was his way, had his door open and had briskly swung himself outside almost before the van had stopped. He lit a cigarette, and with his back to us, contemplated the buildings in front of him.

Feeling suddenly, frighteningly, alert, I asked Na if we were going on to the next site as planned.

'We stay the night here,' she said, suddenly evasive.

My blood began to pound harder. 'I thought we were going to Shangdu.'

'Shangdu is in an army-occupied area, closed to foreigners,' said Na. Then added, 'I myself thought we were going. I did not know it was an army-occupied area.'

'Now the important thing is to stay cool,' said George pleasantly, as I turned on him a look of burning outrage. 'We have come a long way,' he said to Na, and launched into a speech about the deep friendship between us, the lone Western travellers, and them, our hospitable and charming guides.

'What were our special visas for, if not access to a forbidden area?' I demanded, following a more direct line of questioning. Na and Mr Hada exchanged anxious looks. The driver had walked off towards the buildings, while the Director sat insouciantly on the kerb, smoking a cigarette.

'We know you have come a long way,' said Na, faltering. 'We know it has costed you much moneys. I myself, until this moment, did not know that past Duolun was an army-occupied area. And we thought you wanted to see Duolun,' she finished lamely. 'It is a very old, historical town.'

'*This* is where we want to go,' I said angrily, and with a dramatic flourish took from George's hands a map we had brought with us, which I had found in an old archaeological journal.

Na and Mr Hada bent their heads over it, tracing various lines with their fingers. Suddenly Mr Hada began talking excitedly, and looked up at us smiling.

'But this map is of Yenshang-tu, where we just came from. Remember, I pointed out the stream . . . ?'

Slowly, fact by fact was marshalled forth, and my mind, by necessity now more or less functioning and in focus, was forced to recognise that I had declined to get out of the van at the very place I had travelled so far to see.

'"Shangdu" means "head place, high place",' said Na. '"Yuan" means "of the Yuan dynasty". "Yuan Shangdu" means "the capital of the Yuan dynasty".'

So all was settled in tears and laughter. It was determined that we would not spend the night in Duolun as had been planned, but would race back to Shangdu.

'We must hurry,' said George, his photographer's eye ever on the sky. 'The light will be gone.'

Once in the van, the driver called out something over his shoulder and then hunkered down over the wheel.

'He says,' Na called back in turn, 'that he will get us there before the sun goes down!'

Back through town we raced, down along the winding road, which emptied us between the dark hills on to the valley floor. Once on level ground, we roared away until we came to the right-angle turn-off, which we took in a cloud of churning dirt and dust. A narrow stream was crossed, and strange elliptical earthworks passed, before we ground to a halt in the palatial compound of the inner city.

> Saddles off west of the Shan
> Ended our northward trail.
> Along the ancient road
> never a farmer seen.
> But vast flat sands, fine grass, pale green,
> where the Jinlian river's daily rains prevail.
>
> *Feng Zizhen*

The mandate to build Shangdu had come to Khubilai from above, in 1256, from his brother Möngke, the Khaghan who preceded him. Möngke's instructions to his younger brother specifically were to found a city nine *li* northwest of the site that is now Duolun, his plan being to establish a Mongol centre that, like Karakorum, could function as military camp, market-place and palace. The location chosen for the city was charged with symbolism, being both on the fringe of China's northeast borders as well as squarely in the Mongol homelands. The establishment in this region of the official residence of a high-ranking member of the imperial Genghisid line unequivocally indicated to the world the political role to which the Mongolian dynasty aspired; it also indicated a readiness to forego the attempt to 'govern from horseback', and to assume the prerogatives of the sedentary life.

According to Rashīd al-Dīn, a site to the east of an existent town, Keminfu, had initially been chosen, but was abandoned after Khubilai had an ominous dream – in real life as in poetry, the inspiration for Xanadu came from beyond the realm of the senses. Scholars and engineers were consulted and a new site was eventually selected in accordance with the principles of the ancient Chinese art of geomancy, beside a *na'ur*, or pond, in a meadow north of the Luan shui river and south of the Dragon Hill. Rashīd's description of the elaborate pains taken subsequently to drain the *na'ur*, and its resulting effect on the landscape, provides a fascinating insight into how some of the more exotic features characteristically associated with Xanadu came, in reality, into being:

> Now in that country there is a stone which they use instead of firewood [i.e. coal]; they collected a great quantity of this and also of charcoal. Then they filled the *na'ur*, and the spring which fed it, with pebbles and broken bricks and melted a quantity of tin and lead over it until it was firm. They raised it up to a man's height from the ground and built a platform on it. And since the water was imprisoned in the bowels of the earth, it came out in the course of time in other places in meadows some distance away, where it flowed forth as so many springs.

The palace complex was laid out in the form of three squares, each fitting inside the other. The largest, and all-encompassing, delineated the Great Khan's hunting park; the second, situated in the southeast corner of the park, contained the imperial city, while the innermost square, set slightly north of centre within the imperial city, contained the palace enclosure. Beyond the walls was a landscape that, according to contemporary descriptions, was as luxuriant and enticing as that within, a mountain-encircled land covered with forests, particularly pine, that were the haunts of a profusion of birds and animals – wolves, stag, roebuck and leopard. Over the centuries, human habitation depleted and finally exterminated altogether the forests of the area, and hunted the birds and animals out of existence. The result is the barren, majestic sweep of uncontained grass that one traverses today, populated by occasional small settlements of peasants and their livestock and rabbits.

Our van had come to a halt in a roughly square enclosure bounded by uncertain earthen walls some two thousand feet in length on either side. Directly abutting the northern wall stood the sole remaining structure, such as it was, a mud-brick platform standing approximately thirty feet high. A line of jagged but clearly deliberate holes gaped like small caves in the platform at ground level, giving it the appearance of an enormous brick oven. This had been the inner palace enclosure, whose earthen walls, now diminished and covered with turf, once stood as high as sixteen feet, and had been surmounted by turrets in each corner and on either side of its entrance gate.

The mud-brick platform had been the foundation of the imperial palace, Taan ko, or the Pavilion of Great Harmony, which had consisted of five separate halls connected to each other by covered corridors, and fashioned in the shape of an inverted U. This was the palace whose splendour and beauty had been extolled by Marco Polo, who described a 'huge palace of marble and other ornamental stones. Its halls and chambers are all gilded, and the whole building is marvellously embellished and richly adorned.' Architecturally, the palace – as indeed the layout of the city complex as a whole – was Chinese. Yet behind the elaborate walls, embellished by Chinese artisans, and under the bright cobalt and green glazed roof-tiles with their dragon-headed gargoyles, the interior trappings of the palace – the felt hangings, animal skins and carpets – would have been Mongolian.

Facing the palace platform was a rectangular mound of earth that indicated the former site of another, unidentifiable structure. Apart from this, no trace of the original thirty-odd imperial buildings remains, although two stone column bases, almost lost to the grass and weeds that have overgrown them, stand like stumps a short distance beyond the platform, and what appears to have been a cistern can be made out to one side. A child-sized statue depicting a man holding a cup, made of grey stone so badly weathered as to be almost unidentifiable, greets one near the entrance, but this is an interloper of sorts; predating Shangdu by hundreds of years, it was transported to the site in the last century by lamists who established a monastery within easy access of the bricks and stones and other useful building materials furnished by Xanadu's crumbling walls and towers.

Remains of the original thirteenth-century timber that had once reinforced the brickwork of the palace platform were pointed out to me by our driver, who with nimble, irreverent fingers prised out sizeable chips for closer inspection. The jagged holes at ground level, said Na, had been made by local peasants who used them as cellars in which to store their potatoes.

Bricks and turf crumbled beneath my feet as I scrambled to the top of the platform; but no one stopped me, and I was shortly joined by the Director of Cultural Relics himself, who was nonchalantly gathering shards of pottery and occasional chunks of glazed tile. From this vantage point I looked down upon a conglomeration of small ashen mud-brick huts abutting the wall outside the palace city. These were not, as I first imagined, storerooms or similar outlying chambers contemporary with the palace, but were the domicile of the aged peasant couple who had built them, and who came out later to share a watermelon with us. It is their potatoes, presumably, that are safely stored in the Great Khan's cellar.

Taking advantage of the platform's height, I gained my first overview of the walls of the second city in the distance, great earth ramparts spanning 4500 feet on each of its four sides. The sun was low now, and the walls were clearly etched against the grassland by their own shadows. Away on the heights of the guardian mountains to the north, the remains of the Khan's beacon-crowned watch-posts showed as smooth nipple-shaped silhouettes. A strong wind had been blowing all day, but so evenly and consistently as to have assumed an abiding place in the landscape – one would no more wish for the wind to stop than for the grass to turn blue, or the sky to lower.

Rafter upon rafter, the storeyed pavilion
reaches the azure sky,
A picture painted in gold
floating atop seven precious pillars.

Zhou Boqi

The few travel accounts that describe this site had led me to expect that something of the inner city would be intact, but not much more. I had not foreseen that I would be awarded this overview of the city's entire perimeters in discernible and unbroken outline, the blueprint, as it were, of its foundations; nor had I anticipated the surviving sense of containment, of a placed marked off, four square from the surrounding wilderness. Yet here below me was the palace enclosure; and there, darkening all the while, the walls of the imperial city, and farther yet, only barely visible on the horizon, the distant walls of the hunting grounds, once reserved for the exclusive use of Khubilai Khan. The initial scare that we would not get here, the wind, the extraordinary light, the vision of Xanadu at my feet – all this had set my adrenalin racing, and I forgot that I was ill. Indeed, I felt keen, alert, almost on fire.

We left the royal compound just as the sun was going down, intending to get back to our former guesthouse before dark, but a staggering sunset stopped us in our tracks, and we halted again outside the imperial city's western wall. The ground still showed signs here and there of being marshy – perhaps the Great Khan's drainage programme is only now giving way. A flock of cranes rose in clattering flight from a bed of reeds, and taking up their stalwart, timeless flight formation, vanished somewhere towards the sun: Marco Polo, too, had remarked upon the cranes of Xanadu.

'The Khan must have chosen this spot for its light,' said George. The sky was like beaten gold, and no other colour or feature of the landscape was now a factor in the scene before us. What mattered was light – light caught and reflected off the individual blades of grass, light gleaming from the loaded haywain that trundled past us on a dirt track running through the city, light casting shadows on the earthworks. The walls of Xanadu were now dark ridges in the grassy plain, the sky the fiery gold of heat reflected from a furnace. Moments later, there appeared above this radiance a horizontal rainbow in perfect tiers of colour – red, orange, green, blue and indigo, and then up to the roof of heaven, deep violet. Away to the north, the sky remained a benign blue, the hills and the bumps of the Great Khan's watchtowers dark against it. A line of geese in earnest, long-necked silhouette passed overhead, rising suddenly from the western horizon, from the light, and as we exclaimed and pointed, more and then more, as if their arrow-straight lines were being shot from a bow from under the edge of the world, sending them hurtling through space, veering off over our heads.

Long after dark we arrived back at our guesthouse in what we had now learned was the village of Lengqi. I was suddenly tired again. Although I knew I should eat, I could not, and while the others went to have dinner, I turned in to bed. Now the pain of whatever it was I was suffering from took over, and I began to shake so violently that my teeth chattered. My cough, which had become incessant, seemed to cause my brains to hit the roof of my skull. When George came back from dinner, we decided to see how I felt the next morning and determine if we should go back to Xilinhot or stay on here, as our visas permitted us several days on the site. There was only a modest clinic and no telephones, we had learned, in Lengqi.

The next morning, however, the ailment, whatever it had been, was apparently gone, although I still did not wish to eat and felt better sitting up in bed than getting dressed and walking around. The driver and Mr Hada had set out to find petrol so a morning visit to the site was in any case out of the question.

In the mid-afternoon, however, we returned to Shangdu. The day was as clear and blue as it had been the day before, but warm and, shockingly, without wind – the architecture of the houses behind their little protective walls, the treeless, barren landscape and the hectic red cheeks of the people, I had taken as hard evidence that the wind blew every day the sun came up in Inner Mongolia.

> Market place so narrow, you can't gallop a horse;
> With mud that deep, it's easy to get a cart stuck.

Frozen flies gather to fight over the sunlight,
While newly arrived swallows slant to catch the wind.
Evening water-drawing brings hubbub to sandy wells;
Morning cook fires cause the breakup of wooden rafts.
Among local inhabitants it's butter tea for everyone –
Customs are simple and not all that extravagant yet.

While clouds cover the Main Street sun,
Winds blow clear the North Gate sky.
A thousand gutters turn white snow to ice,
And ten thousand cook stoves raise blue smoke.
Middays have been so sultry that I carry a fan,
Though mornings are cold enough to wear a padded gown.
That empty strip through the pines is the boundary,
Trees cut and culled no one knows how many years ago.

Miscellaneous Songs on the Upper Capital

Bypassing the palace enclosure, we determined to devote the afternoon to the outer walls. Whereas there was an air of something tired
and mean in the decay of the inner city, the decline of the outer walls
had produced majestic hulks which, now that we were faced with the
prospect of traversing them on foot, seemed immense. While the
palace city had been reserved expressly for the use of the Great Khan
and his imperial retinue, the function of the inner *huangcheng*, or
imperial city, was administrative, and had accommodated as many as
one hundred thousand inhabitants in mud and board dwellings.
According to legend, over a hundred Buddhist and Taoist temples
and Muslim mosques had also been included in this compound,
reflecting the Great Khan's tolerance of diverse faiths. Its walls may
have formerly been as high as eighteen feet, and between eighteen
to twenty-four feet in thickness, a breadth that has more or less been
retained. The ancient Chinese 'rammed earth' technique had been
used in their construction, and for aesthetic reasons they had been
faced with brick and marble.

Today the cambered, overgrown ridges that rise from dimpled turf resemble barrows on a meadow more than the walls of an imperial city. Striding along the heights of these grassy battlements, one looks down into what would appear to be grazing land, and which was indeed being enjoyed by a flock of sheep that had either wandered in through gaps in the crumbled walls, or used one of the six entrance gates. Each gateway had formerly been strengthened in front by a granite-faced extension decorated with carved lions and dragons. The granite facing has disappeared, but the underlying earthworks have survived and still retain an air of importance, conveying as they do that the lapses in the barrows are deliberate and not an accident of erosion. The extensions of the southern gate in particular are greatly impressive: its wings project outside the city in a swooping V, like extended arms, and cry out for a processional host to embrace. Beyond the gate, the southern walls slope away, almost to ground level, and the marshy ground of the enclosure itself has given way here and there to form stagnant ponds. From out of the eastern wall, where the slender, oblong brickwork underlying the turf is exposed and well-preserved, a twisted tree grew, providing mottled shade.

Some distance to the east, beyond the imperial city, there arose a small, conical and apparently man-made hill which promised to be a good lookout point. As I made my way towards it across the dry grass, I felt a sudden jolt inside me: the vague malaise that had returned after leaving Lengqi had become sharp and had perceptibly shifted from my back to my chest. With the clarity that illness can bestow, I now knew that the problem lay in my lungs.

At the top of the hill, I sat down to rest on parched grass that hummed and cracked with locusts. From here, the palace enclosure and its resilient mud-brick platform, backed by the peasants' huts, was seen to sit humbly within the ponderous earthworks of the imperial city, like a cattleshed within its kraal. Several lines of flattened grass indicated wagon paths, leading casually through Xanadu to somewhere else. A view of the outermost walls that contained the hunting park, which we had yet to visit, now manifested the scale of the city complex as a whole. To the north and south, the walls were clearly apparent as being essentially grander versions of the grassy barrows that we had already traversed; dimly, some miles away on the horizon, one could discern the outermost western wall. To someone arriving cold upon the scene, with no knowledge of Khubilai Khan (or Coleridge's poem), a military encampment might have come to mind – certainly something associated with power. During Khubilai's reign, the complex must have astonished arriving envoys, this Chinese court in a wilderness of barren space, overlooked by beacon-flaming hills. On the opposite side, close to my lookout hill and beyond the eastern outer wall, lay a number of elliptical, caterpillar-shaped mounds. These, like the several moats that have been cut at various points around the city complex, had been built as channels in case of flood; the hills to the north of Shangdu form a watershed in the rainy season and, additionally, the little trickle that is now the Shangdu Gol had in earlier times been a river of sufficient size to enable rafts and flat-bottomed grain junks to ascend to this point from the sea.

Also visible from this vantage point, in the not-distant-enough distance to the west, a clutter of smoke-spewing chimneys betrayed a sprawling village with walls and towers of its own. Some of the chimneys, I was later informed, belonged to the ubiquitous brick kilns that appear to stand in the vanguard of all industrial advancement in Inner Mongolia. I had already heard rumours that the ancient grounds of Shangdu had been scheduled for development into wheat fields, but the presence of the kiln smoke suggests that its fate could be less picturesque.

On coming down the hill, I met up with the rest of the group at our van, which the driver had pulled up under the lone tree on the eastern wall. My skin seemed suddenly paper-fine, and stretched tightly over my bones, as if it suffered from too much sun. I found myself moving carefully, and was glad that we were driving to the outer walls of the hunting park.

Several green elms
extend east of the pavilion,
With its cloud windows and rosy sunset doors
decorated so exquisitely.
The patterned deer in the Upper Park,

taller than horses,
From time to time lead gray-brown fawns,
there in the jade-green grass.

Zhou Boqi

As the inner two enclosures sit in the extreme southeastern corner of the park, the hunting grounds wrap around them to the north and west like a carpenter's square, running one-and-a-half miles long on each side. Although small hunting parks had been features of the imperial grounds of a few Chinese dynasties, the inspiration in this case appears to be native Mongolian, rather than a Chinese precedent. According to Marco Polo, the only entrance into the park, whose walls were as high as twenty feet, was by way of the palace. His description of the Great Khan's pleasure grounds is justly famous:

> [A] wall, running out from the city wall in the direction opposite to the palace, encloses and encircles fully sixteen miles of parkland well watered with springs and streams and diversified with lawns ... Here the Great Khan keeps game animals of all sorts, such as hart, stag, and roebuck, to provide food for the gerfalcons and other falcons which he has here in mew. The gerfalcons alone amount to 200. Once a week he comes in person to inspect them in the mew. Often, too, he enters the park with a leopard on the crupper of his horse ...

The imperial gardens were called *Ruilin*, meaning 'felicitous forest'. No buildings are mentioned by Polo, apart from a collapsible 'palace' constructed of cane, which appears to have been a kind of richly decorated bamboo yurt.

Trundling along the perimeter of the walls in the van, the enclosure seemed immense, and even without the enticement of springs and fountains, running brooks and shaded groves, one could well imagine sauntering on horseback across this naked space. In spite of Marco Polo's assertion that entrance to the park was only made by way of the palace, there were, as in the walls of the imperial city, a number of distinct entranceways; in all likelihood, however, these were made at a later date. From time to time we stopped the van so as to get out and survey the walls. The sun had begun to sink, and I was finding it increasingly difficult to clamber up the grassy slopes of each embankment.

Finally, on the summit of the northwest corner of the outer wall, when we had nearly completed our circuit of the park, I felt my chest clutched more tightly, and knew that my time was up. I gazed into the park one last time, and then slithered down the wall, returned to the van, and stretched out on the back seat. We made one final stop before leaving the site: on the edge of the western wall, the cranes of Xanadu once again put in an appearance, although I did not see them this time, but had to imagine their silhouettes fluttering darkly against the low sun as they rose clattering from the reeds, before assuming the taut line of flight that took them to wherever they disappeared each evening.

Back in Lengqi, we drove straight to the clinic, a modest stone building, largely in darkness as it was officially closed. The yellow bulbs that were clicked on as we passed from room to room left little pools of murky light in the empty halls. I was taken to an examination room and laid down on a mattress of straw stuffed in a white slipcover, while Na, Mr Hada and the Director gathered around my feet, and George took up a position by my head. The doctor came in wearing a blue Mao jacket and the close-lipped, inscrutable ex-pression of a grass-roots Party boss or union chief – used to giving directives, used to having them obeyed, unused to being questioned. My temperature was taken while a blood sample was taken from my earlobe.

'It is 39.9 degrees, Carolina,' said Na. 'You have a fever.'

'What is that in Fahrenheit?' I asked George. 'I don't know what that means,' I said, turning to Na.

'Thirty-seven degrees is normal temperature,' said Na. 'You don't know what that means, but *we* know it is high.'

A nurse in a white robe entered the room and said something, and Na told me I must follow her. I was working out my temperature –

degrees Celsius, times nine, equals nearly 360 – divided by 5, say 71, 72 – plus 32 equals nearly 104 degrees. I was relieved: So I really was ill, so I was right to come here – I had been right to leave Xanadu.

The nurse leads me into a tiny, dim room, empty save for a hulking X-ray machine resembling those in photographs in books about early medicine. My shirt is removed, but not my bra, with the result that the developed X-ray photo shows the two half-moon arcs of the bra's underwire. The doctor taps the negative and nods.

'Pneumonia,' Na translates. I am told that I will be given an injection.

'Is this an antibiotic?' George asks. 'Is this penicillin?'

'It is for her fever,' Na replies, translating the doctor's answer. The injection is given by the nurse, who holds the needle in her fist, draws back so as to gain momentum, and pounds it into my upper thigh with such force that there is a resounding thud as it hits. George laughs with disbelief.

'I am thirsty,' I tell him, and he goes to the van to get the boiled water we have cooled. Na intervenes.

'The doctor says that you must drink hot waters only for your infection. You must wrap yourself in many blankets to make you sweats.' All the faces in the room are looking at me, their expressions exaggerated as if I were seeing them through a fish-eye lens.

'You must sweats,' Na repeats. Her face is doing all the things an Oriental woman's is supposed to do – float like a flower in the night, shine white in the darkness, have dark slashes for eyes. The faces behind her, I realise, are all miming the word 'sweat' in languages I do not understand, running their hands over their brows, shaking their fingers.

'You must sweat, sweat, sweat.' With bewilderment, I feel the blood rush to my face, and am aware that my temperature is rising – does the injection raise it before making it come down? I am drinking the hot water when George returns.

'You must wrap her in many blankets,' Na reiterates. I am confused, for I have a vivid memory of an earlier fever, in Africa. Should I not be lying bare to the air, with strips of cloth dipped in cold water applied to my forehead, my chest, my wrists?

'You must sweats,' Na repeats. 'This injection will make you sweats.'

We return to the Lengqi guesthouse, where I am placed on the big bed I have found so comforting, and Na ensures that I am wrapped in two blankets and a quilt. I lie stock-still throughout the night, dozing off on occasion, but mostly staying awake, dutifully sitting up to drink water, dutifully imagining myself awakening from a deep slumber bathed in perspiration.

'It is strange you are not sweating,' George says cautiously, and I know he is worried. I begin to shake again, and hear my bones rattle, my teeth chatter. My cough returns, and I discover I have become too weak to contain it – it threatens to detonate my skull, to shatter my frame. I end up on my hands and knees, half barking, half gagging.

'You must summon everything you have for this night,' says George. He has been outside, I will discover later, pleading with our entourage to let us return directly to Beijing; we could drive through the night, and be there the next day.

'It is an army-occupied area,' he is told. Our visas are good only as far as Duolun. To return to Beijing, we must drive back to Xilinhot, and wait two days for the next flight out to Hohhot. From Hohhot, we can fly to Beijing. Without a telephone, few advance arrangements can be made.

In the morning, my temperature has fallen one-half a degree Fahrenheit, and the promised sweat has not come. Back at the clinic, I receive another injection in the same distinctive manner as before, and am also given a number of medications, one of which is cough syrup.

We buy a blanket from a local shop, and I am wrapped in this and put in the back of the van. The long return drive on the dirt road is bumpy, but I don't care as I am half in a trance.

In Xilinhot, we first check in with the local hospital, where the diagnosis and treatment of the doctor at Lengqi is confirmed. We then return to the White Horse Hotel, where we had stayed upon arrival. Formerly, we had reached the hotel by turning off the road and driving across a patch of dirt where the grass had been worn away; but the construction of the apartment buildings opposite has proceeded at such a pace that a new way into the hotel has had to be devised, and we circle the area on a makeshift driveway, spiralling inwards.

The new room we are given opens directly on to a factory, whose towering narrow chimneys belch black smoke that seeps in through the windows. The room is too filthy to allow one's mind to settle on any single object – not on the worn lace curtains through which the light struggles; not on the red plush velvet overstuffed chairs and matching television cover; not on the sheets, with their stray unfamiliar black hairs, or on the dingy pillows; not on the stained, burred carpet; certainly on no object in the bathroom – the nicotine-brown tub, the broken tiles that show the swirls of dirt and hair of the last cleaning rag, the non-functioning toilet, the one dim bulb.

Apart from twice-daily visits to the hospital for an injection, I spend the next two days in bed, with the sheets pulled up cautiously over my nose and mouth, so as to filter out as much as possible the chimney smoke and the vaguely fishy odour that permeates the air and which, I discover later, is the smell of the Xilinhot brand of disinfectant. The light in the bedroom is broken, but this does not concern me, as there is nothing that I care to see.

Once, I get out of bed and feebly tidy up the room; the ploy is that a pretence of neatness may, by familiar association, convey an impression of cleanliness. Mostly I lie flat on my back, under carefully arranged covers, and do not move. I think dutifully, carefully, of food; I awake and plan a taste that I can stomach – yoghurt and apples, boiled potatoes with lots of salt. But when the food materialises, it never tastes as I had imagined, and I have to give up after a few mouthfuls. Our entourage is unfailingly kind and sympathetic, Na in particular going beyond the call of duty in her quest to find food that I might want to eat.

My mind refuses to take in my surroundings, and my half-trance intensifies. To remind myself of why I am here, I conjure up in my mind's eye the walls and lost towers of Xanadu. In the night, I have a vision: I am in Xanadu at sunset. There is a glory of light, the flood of gold light reflected from a field of wheat, shining to the aether. Black geese in crisp, black silhouette wing their way in an unending frieze across the heavens; in all the cosmos there is only black earth and gold, heavenly – above all, purifying – fire.

On the third night, I awake in alarm. The thin mattress is soaked through, all the way from top to bottom. I touch myself, and with amazement discover that I am the cause. I am in a cold sweat that will soak through two additional pairs of sheets; but the fever has broken.

Our flight to Hohhot is the next day. While lying in this room, I have missed a number of events. The Director has held a great feast and there has been a local dance at the White Horse Hotel. I am sorry not to have taken advantage of this hospitality; but now the moment of departure has arrived, I at last admit to myself that I loathe the place and am ready to flee.

On the morning of departure, I have a final injection and then we drive to the airport. Our goodbyes are warm, and the Director gives us each a blue prayer shawl and bestows on George his Genghis Khan tiepin.

We board the plane, and for the first time in my life, I regard the prospect of flying with no apprehension – if I were meant to have been finished off on this trip, it would surely have happened by now. For weeks afterwards I will have motion sickness as a side-effect of one of the prescribed drugs: I have been taking, unawares, three separate massive courses of antibiotics, one of which is used for treatment of bone-marrow infections.

The plane trundles out for takeoff on Chinese time, which is to say exactly on schedule. The propellers spin, the plane shakes and rattles, then pulls away, slipping on the grassy runway. Clouds of locusts whir out of the brittle, gold grass as we advance, and then, strangely, follow the plane, perhaps attracted by its heat. We slowly rise, and through the window beside me I watch the wheels pull up, and we have left the grass and locusts behind.

The reign of the Great Khan Khubilai represented the height of Mongol power, indeed, arguably, one of the high-water marks of world history. Among the distinctive achievements of his rule were the refinement of a communications network throughout his empire, which, by the end of his reign, had established fourteen hundred postal stations in China. Khubilai paved roads, and renovated the Great Canal which runs eleven hundred miles from Hangzhou to Beijing. Traditional Chinese literary as well as fine arts benefited from his patronage, with the most notable advances being the resurgence of the theatre and the development of the novel. Similarly, the study of medicine and science flourished under his far-sighted regard; two branches of imperial hospitals, staffed primarily with Muslim doctors, were established in Shangdu and north China, Persian astronomers were invited to his court and in 1271, the Institute of Muslim Astronomy was founded in Dadu.

Khubilai's health had never been particularly good – it is recorded, for instance, that in 1269 he had sent to Korea for special fish-skin shoes to relieve his gouty feet – but from 1279 onwards, it began to worsen, exacerbated by the heavy drinking in which it seems all of the Khans indulged. His various ailments took not only a personal toll on the ageing Khan, but were to have disastrous repercussions on the management of his empire. A number of his ministers, most notably his finance minister, were convicted of crimes of graft and exploitation of the Khan's Chinese subjects. With affairs at home threatening to get out of control, Khubilai lost some of his characteristic tolerance and issued anti-Muslim edicts, perhaps partly in reaction to the dominance by Muslim states to the west over Mongol allies, perhaps also because many of the ministers who had betrayed his trust were Muslim.

In 1281, Khubilai's favourite wife Chabi died, and in 1286 he was struck yet another blow with the death of his son, Chen-chin, whom he had carefully groomed to be his successor. His biographer, Morris Rossabi (from whose book most of the details of Khubilai's personal life have been taken), suggests that these personal tragedies marked the beginning of the Great Khan's end. His court became increasingly lavish, possibly due to the fact that Chabi, who had been a byword for frugality, was no longer around to exert her influence. Increasingly, he turned to heavy bouts of eating and drinking and, to quote Rossabi, 'grew obese and suffered from ailments associated with alcoholism'.

Abroad as well as at home, the Great Khan suffered disastrous setbacks. An attempt to invade Japan in 1281 (and avenge the failure of an earlier invasion) ended dismally with the loss of an estimated 130,000 allied and enemy lives. Campaigns in South Asia resulted in similar, if less spectacular, losses. Rebellions in Tibet and Manchuria, outlying regions of the Khan's empire, in the 1280s and early 1290s, indicated that the Great Khan was losing his grip.

Chinese sources state that by 1294, Khubilai, by now dangerously obese, was exhausted and depressed. The *Yuanshih*, or history of the Yuan dynasty, notes that an old comrade-in-arms arrived in court with the hope of raising his spirits, but did not succeed. Finally, on 18 February 1294, at the age of eighty, the Great Khan died in the Zitan, or Hall of Purple Sandalwood, of his Dadu palace. His body was buried somewhere in the Hentiyn Mountains east of Karakorum, although exactly where and in what manner has never been determined. Posthumously, he was awarded by his officials the title *Shizu*, or 'Founder of a dynasty'; to the Mongols, he was always *Setzan Khan* – the Wise Khan – and they surely would have deemed him worthy of Coleridge's dream-poem. Khubilai's grandson, Temür, by his favourite, lost son Chen-chin, was his immediate successor. The Yuan emperors of China were to hold sway until 1370 and, in all, ten successors of Khubilai's house would sit upon his imperial throne in Dadu.

While Shangdu continued to be used as a summer residence by the Yuan emperors who followed Khubilai, it appears to have eventually lost the cachet of being a capital city, although some vestige of its original importance is indicated by the fact that it was the site of the enthronement of a number of later emperors. Its official stature lost, the former upper capital was apparently transformed into a private pleasure area. Certainly it was primarily as a hunting ground that it was enjoyed by the successive Khans. It was also the case that other summer palaces were built in the same area later in the Yuan dynasty – clearly the proximity to the great grasslands of the steppes continued to attract the Mongol emperors.

Glimpses may be caught of the later history of the summer palace in the *Zezhi tongjian houbian* (or *Supplement to Comprehensive Mirror to Aid in Government*), which includes a chronicle of events of this region over the thirteenth and fourteenth centuries. We read, for instance, that one night in 1301, the northwestern portion of the city was flooded by heavy rains; that 1321 was a year of ambitious building – a *dian*, or hall, was erected in honour of a certain lama, a golden tower was constructed for the holy remains of a Buddhist monk and the city wall was improved and strengthened. Two years later, strangely, all gold- and silverwork ceases in Shangdu. In 1354, an imperial order was given to lay a stone road from Dadu, leading north to Shangdu. And in 1358, in a war of rebellion, Shangdu was invaded by the *Hongjin*, or 'red-capped bandit' forces of Guan Duo, who occupied the city for seven days, set the palace in flames and then moved on. Shangdu continued to be inhabited for some decades longer, but ceased to be frequented by the Khans.

The Yuan empire had been critically weakened by the domestic and military crises of Khubilai's later years. None of the subsequent Khaghans proved as able a statesman as had he, and the internal decay that had been set in motion under his reign progressively worsened. The Mongol power base was further eroded by factional infighting, and real authority ended up in the hands of individual warlords, not of the emperor. In the 1330s and later, in the 1350s, a wave of natural disasters that included flood and outbreaks of pestilence (possibly bubonic plague, which originated in Mongol territory) further weakened the demoralised empire. From the time they had assumed power, the Mongols had excluded themselves from taxation, and had essentially lived off the Chinese peasantry, thus provoking an economic and social imbalance that had long been resented. Now, in the 1340s, small- and large-scale rebellions, especially in the south, which had always been less than securely held, haphazardly broke out among the disgruntled Chinese peasants. When, finally, in 1368, an organised assault was led by one of the peasant leaders, the Mongol forces had neither strength nor wits enough to stave them off.

The last Khan, Toghon Temür, who had assumed the imperial

Zezhi tongjian houbian, or Supplement to Comprehensive Mirror to Aid in Government.

throne at the age of thirteen, fled Dadu in 1368, and made for the steppes and Shangdu, where he held out briefly, before being decisively defeated the following year. The Chinese troops entered the summer palace, took as prisoners the children of the city's important officials and fired the city a second time. In Dadu, power was assumed by the bandit rebel Zhu Yuanzhang, who had led the successful rebellion, and who installed himself as the first of the Ming emperors. Thus was the Yuan, the shortest-lived of China's major dynasties.

From 1370, Shangdu served essentially as a border post manned by Chinese forces, from where an eye could be kept on the movements of the Mongols to the north, who continued to conduct a campaign of unabated if futile and disorganised harassment. Toghon Temür died of an illness the same year in Karakorum, the first official Mongolian palace, to which he had continued his flight for sanctuary. Sanang Setzen, the poetical historian of the Mongols, commemorated the loss of the last of the Yuan emperors by putting into his mouth the following lament:

> My vast and noble Capital, my Dadu, my
> splendidly adorned.
> And Thou, my cool and delicious Summer
> seat, my Shangdu ...
> Ye also, yellow plains of Shangdu, Delight
> of my godlike Sires.
> I suffered myself to drop into dreams –
> and lo! My Empire was gone.

In 1430, five years into the reign of the fifth Ming emperor, the northern frontier was contracted to the line of the Great Wall, and the garrison that had been posted at Shangdu was moved south to Dushikou. With its removal, Shangdu ceased to exist as a vital centre, and became one of a number of deserted ruins on the outposts of the Chinese empire.

Over the centuries, the abandoned site was visited by only a handful of travellers who left reports. In 1691, a French Jesuit, John Françoise Gerbillon, paid a short visit to Shangdu in the course of accompanying the then Chinese emperor on a hunting trip. Gerbillon offers no description of the site, other than remarking that the ruins of Shangdu lay in a plain by a little river; but the account is interesting for the evidence it provides that the area was still enjoyed by imperial hunting parties, and that it maintained, at this date at least, a vestige of its formerly abundant game: Gerbillon states that leopard, tigers, stags, roebuck, mountain goats, fox, hares and boar were encountered by his party.

In 1872, Reverend Stephen Wootton Bushell of the British Legation in Peking, en route from Peking north to Dolonnur, made a day trip to the site, which was by this time locally known as Chzhun'-nayman-sume, or the City of One Hundred and Eight Temples, a nod to the former glory of the Great Khan's city. He found the walls of the city, 'built of earth, faced with unhewn stones and brick', still standing, but in a dilapidated state. Over the entrance gate to the palace enclosure, however, there rose 'a perfect arch 20 feet high, 12 feet wide'. The platform which had centuries before served as the foundation of the Great Khan's palace, described by Bushell as a 'bare square earth fort, faced with brick', had been decorated with 'the usual ragged streamers of silk and cotton tied to sticks'; these Bushell took as evidence of the 'superstitious regard' with which the Mongols continued to regard the site, but they may in fact have indicated its use by Buddhist lamas as a temple. The foundations of some of the other buildings that had formerly stood in the palace enclosure could still be traced in the overgrown grass. The ground was strewn with blocks of marble, and 'broken lions, dragons, and the remains of other carved monuments' lay scattered haphazardly in the tangled overgrowth. The best preserved artefact was a broken memorial tablet 'in an ancient form of the Chinese character, surrounded by a border of dragons boldly carved in deep relief'. Bushell's account dwells upon the sense of desolation that pervaded the abandoned scene, and on the brooding landscape of volcanic hills and rolling prairie, the 'rank weeds', the foxes, owls, prairie rats and partridges that had inherited the site.

A more extensive, but no less bleak, description was given by a Russian traveller, Andreev Pozdneev, who passed through in 1898 –

Pozdneev was no casual visitor, but had been the chief archaeologist of the earliest Mongolian palace in Karakorum. Arriving near dark at the end of a rainy day, he endured a miserable night in a wet tent before venturing out at daybreak the following drizzling morning. Unlike Bushell, whose exploration seems to have been confined to the palace enclosure, Pozdneev doggedly paced the sodden outer walls, which he found in general well-preserved, commenting that 'in some places they stand so sturdily and are so undamaged that it is difficult to believe that these ruins have survived five centuries'. He, too, found a quantity of glazed tiles as well as decorations carved in granite; the Chinese inscription described by Bushell was still intact, and even 'beautifully polished'. Vertical beams of the round towers that had once stood guard in the corners of the wall of the second, imperial city still remained, and in the northeast corner were significant ruins of the tower itself.

Within the palace enclosure Pozdneev found a mishmash of foundation lines and rubble. More clear-eyed than Bushell, he sums up his observations by declaring that 'it is absolutely pointless to set forth my conclusions about the functions of all these buildings and their parts, or the various sections of the city . . . without a doubt, not a single hill here looks the way it would have in the Yuan capital; because on all these ruined buildings, already more than once, new structures were built up, of which are now preserved only ruins and disordered mounds of refuse.' He goes on to cite the Chinese garrison, the transient Chinese merchants who built sheds for trade, the nomads who put up fences and walls with the remaining stones as pens for their sheep and camels. Perhaps more telling than the neglect and mistreatment of the physical ruins is the ignorance of his Mongolian companions regarding the former palace of one of their greatest countrymen, an ignorance that Pozdneev bitterly mocks:

> The local Mongolians, according to legends, know that Chzhun'-nayman-sume was the capital of Kublah, they even show the place where his palace stood; but, skipping over the most important periods of changes in Chzhun'-nayman-sume, i.e. the Ming dynasty, they go on to tell in great detail about how

here lived a regiment of Chinese soldiers in the time of the Khans and with naive surprise will assure the listener of the great artistic capabilities of these soldiers, who had built enormous barracks inside the city wall, using its bricks.

Only four years later, in 1902, another Englishman made his way to the ruins. Charles William Campbell, the British Consul at Wuzhou, published his brief comments in an official report he wrote for the Foreign Office regarding a journey he had taken through Mongolia. Campbell had read Bushell's report (but evidently not Pozdneev's, which was only published in Russian), and professed that he had 'nothing of importance to add to Dr Bushell's description'. He went on to add offhandedly, however, the striking fact that since Bushell's visit, 'some vandal lamas have collected most of the interesting marbles and stone work and made an *obo* of them'. At this time, the enduring arch of the great southern entrance, 'under which Khubilai himself must have passed frequently', still stood, as Bushell described, but shows 'signs that the ruins were being drawn upon for building materials'. The final line of his report may prove prescient: 'As soon as the line of Chinese immigration invades this part of the Shangtu Valley, the disappearance of these interesting ruins will be a matter of a very few years.'

The reports so far mentioned were the result of fleeting visits, but in 1925, Lawrence Impey, an American diplomat in Peking, spent an entire month in the remains of the palace complex. His thorough and methodical measurements of the walls and earthworks resulted in a twenty-one-page article, complete with a map of the ancient city and cross-sections of the remaining walls, in the American *Geographical Review*. Impey's journey from Peking to the site took him along the ancient route used by the Khans, and he remarks that 'all the way up, from the Nankow Pass above Peking to the last miles of marshland that bring one into the ruins of Shangtu, one finds watchtowers that guarded the trail'. In essence, his detailed description reveals that little had changed since the visit of the last traveller. He notes, however, that 'the arch of the southern gate has now collapsed', although its remains are clearly defined. He observed that a great quantity of blue and green glazed tiles was to be found in the wall, evidence that 'the Great Khan had his kilns on the site and that the throwouts not used for roofing were dumped into the wall work'. These colourful tiles were doubtless particularly attractive to later scavengers in search of novel building materials. Impey found a mass of tiles, pottery and stonework, which he carefully catalogued according to where each piece was discovered, and concluded his article with the plea that, especially in view of the recent discoveries by Russian excavators in Karakorum, 'it would be well worth the while of some museum to take up the quest at the point where the author was forced from want of time and money to relinquish it'.

Impey's plea was answered, in part, in July of 1937, when a team of six Japanese archeologists representing 'the Archaeological Seminar in the Faculty of Letters of Tokyo Imperial University' arrived at the site. The party set up camp near an abandoned lama temple 'of recent construction', which had been erected upon the rectangular mound that now blankly faces the palace platform within the inner city. From here, guarded by eleven Mongolian soldiers, they conducted a week-long investigation. The result of their sojourn is a weighty publication, in Japanese, with extensive photographs of the site and of the artefacts haphazardly referred to by the other reports – the milky blue and green pottery, the stonework embossed with rosettes, lotus blossoms and floral scrolls, the grinning lion jambs, the florid turquoise-and-gold dragon's heads, the chips of gold-leafed lacquer images, the inscribed steles, the cobalt, green, yellow and rich brown-glazed tiles, the roof *shibis*, the monumental carved tortoise used as a base to support imperial inscriptions, the stone lion.

The map of the ruined city drawn by these archaeologists does not differ significantly from that drawn by Impey, whom they cite, noting that his survey and report were 'tolerably correct'. Instead of retreading old ground, therefore, they devoted themselves to other tasks. No actual spadework was implemented by this archaeological team; rather, they contented themselves with gathering up 'whatever tiles, bricks, pottery and stone objects we could find on the surface of the ground' – in short, everything that wasn't nailed down – and the considerable fruits of their labour were then shipped to the Tokyo

Imperial University, and it is there, presumably, that the treasures of Shangdu still survive. Thus, when in 1988 a British traveller, William Dalrymple, managed to obtain an all too brief glimpse of the inner palace enclosure, through dusk and driving rain, while in the process of being deported from the forbidden area by Mongolian authorities, there were, for him as shortly afterwards for us, no artefacts of note remaining to be seen.

A melancholy tone pervades the descriptions left by the British and American travellers to Shangdu. All of them had been led to the site by 'Kubla Khan', and all refer to the poem in their reports. Like me, they must have known in advance that the fallen walls of this Chinese military garrison in the wasteland of the Mongolian steppes would bear little resemblance to the Xanadu of poetic legend. Yet, apparently, the disparity between the poetic vision and the archaeological reality took them all unawares.

For my part, I had come to see that the Great Khan and his summer place of pleasure possessed a certain romantic magnetism of their own, without benefit of Coleridge's poem. The sight of Shangdu rising from the shadows of its ruins as the light subsided had exposed the surviving grandeur of this barren land, denuded as it was of its walls and towers, gardens, ancient forests and rills. Nonetheless, this was not the landscape that had first inspired me. And now, at journey's end, I was struck with a yearning for a glimpse of the poetic vision.

Where did the Xanadu of Coleridge's imagination, and subsequently of ours, arise? The ostensible source, and that cited by Coleridge, is Purchas' *Pilgrimage*, an early seventeenth-century compendium of famous travel stories and histories. It was a special favourite of Coleridge, who was a voracious reader of literature of this genre. The relevant passage, which is essentially a crib from Marco Polo's account, reads as follows:

> In *Xamdu* did *Cublai Can* build a stately Palace, encompassing sixteene miles of plaine ground with a wall, wherein are fertile

Meddowes, pleasant springs, delightfull Streames, and all sorts of beasts of chase and game, and in the middest thereof a sumptuous house of pleasure, which may be removed from place to place. Here he doth abide in the months of June, July, and August, and on the eight and twentieth day wherof, he departeth thence to another place to do sacrifice ...

This excerpt clearly reveals the inspiration for the pleasure palace, the walls, the fertile ground and the rills and streams of 'Kubla Khan'. On the other hand, some of the poem's most memorable imagery is strikingly absent – there is no mention of a sacred river, for example, or of incense-bearing trees, a cedarn cover, a mighty fountain, or a cave of ice. Looking no further than Purchas, one would have to conclude that the Xanadu of the poem was indeed largely a place of the imagination.

In 1927, John Livingston Lowes, an eminent scholar of English literature, published a critical examination of Coleridge's poetic methods entitled *The Road to Xanadu*. In this landmark book, Lowes demonstrated that the imagery of 'Kubla Khan' was derived from a variety of literary sources in addition to those specifically mentioned by Coleridge. Throughout his life, it had been Coleridge's habit to keep a running Notebook, in which he jotted down his preoccupations of the moment, whether they were domestic occurrences, unpaid bills, his daily schedule or books that he was reading. It is the latter entries that are of most interest, for they contain a record of the works that had fed Coleridge's imagination prior to the composition of his poetic masterpiece; a record that in view of the singular and unpremeditated manner in which the poem was supposed to have 'happened' is of surpassing value. Coleridge could be very precise when making his literary notations, entering not merely book titles or authors' names, but specific pages or passages, often copied out, that had caught his fancy. It is in these pages, as Lowes notes, that one may 'catch glimpses of the strange and fantastic shapes which haunted the hinterland of Coleridge's brain ... what the teeming chaos of the Note Book gives us is the charged and electrical atmospheric background of a poet's mind'.

The list of books that contributed their imagery, diction or reso-
nance to 'Kubla Khan' is impressively diverse, ranging from Pausanias
to Milton, and from mythological to scientific treatises. This rich
variety notwithstanding, Lowes demonstrates definitively that the
poem's most dominant imagery can be attributed to a small nucleus
of books of travel and discovery. In many cases, the familiar but
incomplete images that shimmer disjointedly from these specific
works, by virtue of their striking similarity, overlapped – or, to use
Lowes' terminology, formed hooks and eyes – in Coleridge's mind
and melded in a single poetic vision. Thus the mystical landscape of
Xanadu, improbably but incontrovertibly, was shaped by descriptions of four distinct geographical regions of the earth.

Lowes's research, then, hinted at an exciting possibility. If it were
true that behind each dream-image there lay a real place that had
been visited and described by a traveller of another age, then this
magnificent poem was less a tribute to the Mongol khan, or to the
powers of poetic imagination, than it was to the inspirational splen-
dours of the earth. And although it was not possible to travel to the
Xanadu of 'Kubla Khan', one might be able to traverse its landscape.

My illness in Nei Menggu had taught me that romantic quests can
run up against hard realities. This quest, however, seemed to me to be
already under way, past the point of turning back. Simply put, the
landscape of Xanadu had haunted me since childhood, and if I were
to behold it, there was not one, but four journeys to be made.

THE
MIGHTY
FOUNTAIN

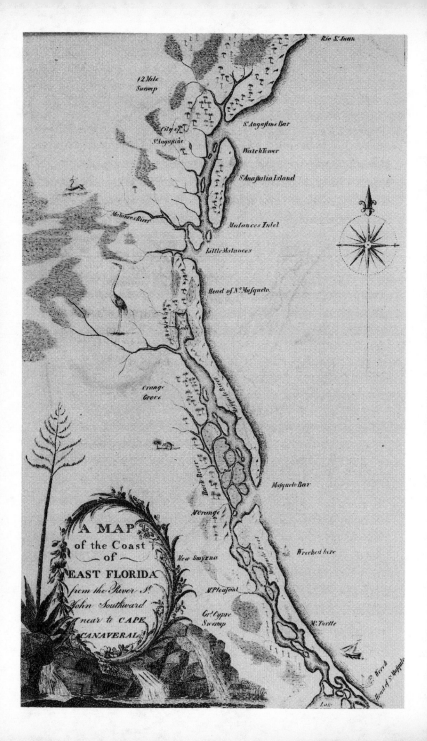

Rio S.t Juan

12 Mile
Swamp

St. Augustine Bar

City of
S.t Augustine

Watch Tower

S.t Anastatia Island

Matances River

Matances Inlet

Little Matances

Head of N.o Musqueto.

Orange
Grove

Musqueto Bar

M.t Orange

Wrecked here

New Smyrna

M.t Pleasant

M.t Turtle

Gr.t Cypre
Swamp

A MAP
of the Coast
of
EAST FLORIDA
from the River S.t
John Southward
near to CAPE
CANAVERAL

Wreck
Head of S.t Augustine

Lake

The Mighty Fountain

In 1932, the first of the Weissmuller *Tarzan* films burst upon the public. The inspiration to do a remake of the original 1918 version of Edgar Rice Burroughs's well-known story about the lost son of an English lord who grows up to be a kind of Khubilai Khan of the African jungle owed much to the success of *Trader Horn*, which two years earlier had been nominated for an Academy Award for the best feature film. The most compelling aspect of *Trader Horn* had been its spectacular and unprecedented wildlife footage, which had been shot in five different African countries. The excitement and curiosity aroused by these startling new images were what the *Tarzan* film-makers hoped to exploit – indeed, footage left over from the earlier movie was incorporated into the Tarzan films.

Although the films today are regarded more as high camp than authentic African adventure, they have their compelling images. The sight of Weissmuller, the greatest swimmer in the world at the time, ploughing through the black jungle water, is itself reason enough for watching; and the underwater sequence in *Tarzan and His Mate* (in which Maureen O'Sullivan was nude in the original uncut version) is a haunting vision in black and white – two white bodies gleaming surreally in filtered sunlight against the inky darkness of the water, like holograms free-floating in space.

The filming of these sequences was, as would be expected, arduous. The stars, largely unprotected by clothing of any note, had to clamber and frolic through rough bush, swim in water infested with giant reptiles and literally put themselves out on a limb for the benefit of the cameras. The crew too suffered – from the muggy heat, the insects, and the difficulty of moving around in the dense undergrowth.

The films reveal little of these inconveniences, as the handsome stars appear always well groomed and unscathed, and the bush is shown to such advantage as to appear almost pastoral. The water of the rivers and lagoons, dark as it is in the black-and-white film, is always clear as a crystal spring; cosy nests are easily built in the majestic, vine-hung trees, and the sunlight on the epiphytes that cloak the forest gives the trees themselves a pleasant woolliness. These epiphytes are sometimes fluttering ragged leaves, and sometimes, if one looks closely, Spanish moss – for the Tarzan films were not made in Africa, but in north Florida.

The same exotic and luxuriant landscape that inspired the vision of a jungle paradise also provided 'Kubla Khan' with some of its most dominant imagery. Coleridge's attention was drawn to this part of the world by the work of William Bartram, an American naturalist and writer who travelled extensively in the southeastern states in the mid-to-late eighteenth century. Bartram was born in 1739, in Pennsylvania, the son of John Bartram, called by Linnaeus 'the greatest natural botanist in the world', and often considered to be the father of American botany. The botanical garden of the senior Bartram, outside Philadelphia, was world famous, and no doubt contributed to his son's passion for the more exotic examples of what he termed 'the vegetable world'. John Bartram had made expeditionary trips for botanical purposes into the Allegheny mountains, North and South Carolina and the Ontario wilderness, and in 1765–6, accompanied by his son, he ventured into Florida. This excursion with his father was the incentive for William's later solitary journey throughout the American South, made between 1773 and 1777. His account of his travels, published in 1791, six years before the composition of 'Kubla Khan', made him famous, and was entitled *Travels through North & South Carolina, Georgia, East & West Florida, the Cherokee Country, the Extensive Territories of the Muscogulges, or Creek Confederacy, and the Country of the Chactaws.*

Coleridge was not alone in being captivated by Bartram's account of the South's luxuriant landscape. The *Travels* was a singular inspiration for the Romantics, and its images were insinuated, in lesser degrees, into the works of Wordsworth, Southey, Shelley, Thomas Campbell, Tennyson and Emerson. While part of the charm of the *Travels* can be ascribed to the southeast's extraordinarily exotic landscape, much credit must go to Bartram's inimitably exuberant presentation of this enchanting world. The heat, the insects, the potentially hostile Seminoles, the encounters with rampaging alligators – none of these dismay Billy Bartram, or detract from his rapturous survey of this corner of the Almighty's globe.

'How glorious the powerful sun, minister of the Most High, in the rule and government of this earth, leaves our hemisphere, retiring from our sight beyond the western forests!' exclaims Bartram on an evening in this Florida June of 1774, when the temperature would have raged somewhere in the muggy nineties. 'I behold with gratitude his departing smiles, tinging the fleecy roseate clouds, now riding far away on the Eastern horizon . . . '

Bartram has been called the first interpreter of the American landscape, and the attribute is significant. It was the uncritical, almost wilful naïvety of Bartram's vision of the southern wilderness that made his narrative so congenial to Romantic armchair explorers. Neither exploits nor mishaps are embellished for the sake of narrative drama; Bartram's self-prescribed role is that of a humble observer of Nature's bounty, not its heroic conqueror, and as a consequence the land he rhapsodises appears in a largely benign light. This vision of the wilderness in which the savagery – and even discomfort – of Nature is largely absent is in many respects not unlike the idyllic tropical jungles of the *Tarzan* films. Both the book and the films seduce their audiences into dreaming of a lost Eden, of a fresh and sparkling world still innocent and untrammelled by humanity.

The north Florida connection with 'Kubla Khan' was a matter of more than passing interest to me, as for the first twenty years of my life I lived less than half an hour's drive from Wakulla Springs, one of the two sites chosen to represent Africa in the *Tarzan* films. When my parents first emigrated from England to this part of the world in the early fifties, they had, I think, imagined perhaps not a Utopia, but a land somewhat similar to the *Tarzan*/Bartram Eden – an exotic wilderness not entirely savage, and admissible of human habitation. They knew that the part of Florida to which they were moving would not be like Miami, the only place in Florida about which much was known in England, and they expected a frontier.

They had first lived in Gainesville, some sixty miles northwest of the site that had provided for Coleridge, by way of Bartram, the imagery for the 'incense-bearing trees', the 'mighty fountain' and the river 'meandering with a mazy motion' of 'Kubla Khan'. Arriving in August of 1955, my mother had travelled south from New York by air-conditioned train, which had not prepared her for the heat that met her like a furnace blast when the doors opened at the Gainesville railway station. Her first impression of Florida was that she had arrived in the midst of an accident – that a terrible fire was raging somewhere around the station.

Shortly afterwards, my parents moved to Tallahassee and settled in following the traditional protocol of all good colonialists. I was registered at birth with the British Consulate, as I would have been had I been born in, say, Timbuctoo. We took the London *Times* in the special airmail edition printed on tissue-thin paper and at night we listened to the BBC World News on our short-wave 'wireless'. Not until I was in junior high school, and faced with a social science project that entailed reading about local civic affairs, did I discover that the *Tallahassee Democrat* was the newspaper of choice of my fellow townsfolk.

This illusion of colonial self-containment could have been perpetrated in very few other places in America. The frontiers of the west, for example, have their own, deeply American mythologies. But we were in the tropics, or the subtropics, and were surrounded at every turn by phenomena that were recognisable only from the travel accounts and popular lore regarding Africa, the Indies, Malaya, India – all the great outposts of the Empire. Our windows were screened against mosquitoes, as they had been in Jamaica (where we briefly lived), as they would have been in Africa; and, for the same reason, the last case of malaria in Florida was as late as 1948. Enormous cockroaches walked boldly about the houses, as they had done in Jamaica, as one believed they would do in Malaya or Borneo. In the rainy season of the summers, grass grew so quickly that our garden could be overgrown in a week; in the springtime, it was ablaze with pink azaleas, wisteria, dogwood and magnolia. The distinctiveness of our surroundings was continually reinforced by my parents' bemused, incredulous or awed comparisons: from domestic concerns, such as the lack of real tea and bread, to the disconcerting confidence and *savoir-faire* of even the youngest natives – at every turn the gulf between the normative world represented by England and this new 'posting' was driven home.

My sister and I spent our childhood being told to 'be careful': the coarse grass ('not a real lawn') harboured snakes. Rabies was – and is – endemic, and every raccoon, possum, stray dog and squirrel was regarded by us, if not by our more acclimatised neighbours, with great circumspection. In the summer, un-air-conditioned houses, and there were many then, fell prey to mildew, which speckled the walls and woodwork. These considerations, compounded by the heat and – above all – the humidity, of which there was no bare conception back in England, were crosses borne by all of us who found ourselves stationed, in whatever part of the globe, in remote tropical outposts.

Wakulla Springs lies fifteen miles south of downtown Tallahassee, and is the centrepiece of what is now a 2900-acre state park. The spring itself is one of the largest in the world, emitting six hundred thousand gallons of water a minute into a basin that is two hundred and fifty feet at its deepest point, and four-and-a-half acres in area. One of the reasons Wakulla was chosen for location shooting of *Tarzan* (and other less well-known films) was that, in addition to looking more like Africa than Africa, its water is some of the clearest in the world, and therefore ideal for underwater photography.

Throughout my childhood, a trip to Wakulla was never a casual outing, but more akin to an expedition. Inevitably, one arrived at the springs through the Wakulla Lodge, a mildly up-market hotel set in grounds abounding with live-oak, magnolia and pine, which roll down an incline to the chainlink fence that marks off the swimming area and the springs. But even with these inescapable elements of domestication at one's back, one looked through the fence to confront the wilderness.

The spring basin was ringed with forest, its true shoreline never entirely discernible behind the vanguard of bleached cypress trees and broken knees that rose starkly from the water, which was itself always dark and coloured by the weather – forest green on sunny mornings, deep blue when the sun was high, and almost black when it was overcast. Birds of prey called from the trees, and above them black buzzards drifted in endless languid circles, causing one always to wonder what they had spotted hidden in the forest reaches.

To one's right, the springs narrowed to form the six-mile-long outflowing Wakulla river that wends its way between jungle-covered banks to the Gulf of Mexico. To one's left was the great, deep basin of the spring, and reached by a decaying catwalk, a wicked-looking thirty-foot diving tower of gaunt and corroding steel. The triumph of diving Tarzan-like into primeval depths provoked a very special kind of joy; but it was also true that people had drowned in the unfathomable underwater caves beneath the tower and that our neighbour (the father of my Mongolian contact, John Olsen) had mastodon bones which he had gathered from these deeper recesses of the springs.

Adjacent to the chainlink fence, a thin strip of sand served as a beach, while a stone's cast away alligators sunned themselves on the opposite shore. Generally, these creatures live peaceably with the visitors, but there have been mishaps, and as recently as 1987, the tourist jungle-boat, on one of its regular cruises up the river, glided past something that was taken at first to be the carcass of a deer, but which closer inspection revealed to be a very different kind of animal; and thus it was discovered that fifteen miles from the centre of a state capital, in the most industrialised nation on earth, a human being had been devoured alive by an alligator.

'I am getting Sick and tired of F[lorid]a,' wrote a farmer to his friend in 1852, the day after a severe storm. 'This is the worst Country that I Ever Lived in and it seems if I Make anything on this Plantation it is distroyed of Late years by the heavy Rains and Stormes ... I have understood that Tallahassee is tetotialy Ruined.'

While the gentler aspects of the landscape – the soft air, the extravagance of flowers – were obviously the most seductive, I also took a kind of perverse comfort in its harsher elements. The greatest threat to any environment, after all, is man, against whom the power of Nature presents a welcome counterforce. Thus, when vast tracts of forest were needlessly ploughed up to make way for yet one more gimcrack apartment block, or for a new shopping mall when old ones lay empty, it was a solace of sorts to know that these too would in time be worn down by the elements and reclaimed by the uncontainable land. The lightning and thunder that rattled our house, the storms that whipped the Spanish moss around the oak limbs, the hurricanes and tornadoes, the pounding torrents of the rainy season – all of these reinforced my romantic belief that I lived in an exotic wilderness.

My sensibilities to this land were thus admittedly extreme, shaped, after all, less by the common pride that everyone here possesses for his surroundings, than by the awe of the resident outsider: a colonialist's appreciation of living in a part of the world that other people – like Coleridge – would only ever read about. From the diving platform at Wakulla Springs, past the dark inlet into which Weissmuller dived from the shaggy, vine-entangled tree, overlooking the cruise-boat pier and swimming buoys, I used to look down a river that, for me, led to Africa, or to somewhere like Africa about which I had yet to learn, and it may well be that my predisposition to travel derived in great part from my belief that I was already 'out there'.

> . . . And there were gardens bright with sinous rills,
> Where blossomed many an incense-bearing tree;
> And here were forests ancient as the hills,
> Enfolding sunny spots of greenery . . .

In our garden in the late afternoon, sunlight fell fuzzily through the Spanish moss that draped the canopy of great oak boughs overhead. From our house, it was possible to look around the neighbourhood and see the remnants of Bartram's world looming behind the other houses in our street. I was still in high school when I first learned that the landscape of north Florida had inspired Xanadu, and I nodded to myself at the discovery. Walking home on a spring evening when the scent of honeysuckle and gardenias hung heavy in the humid air; or gingerly crossing our coarse lawn, harsh and blinding green in the sun; or diving into Wakulla's forest encircled depths – the uninitiated might be surprised at the connection, but I well understand how Florida furnished Xanadu with its incense-bearing trees, its sunny spots of greenery, its underwater caverns measureless to man. Previously, I had felt no interest in the specific places Coleridge had read about – my own vision had no need of them. But faithful to my quest, I was now prepared to seek them out.

For Coleridge, Bartram's *Travels* was not a casual find, but a work that he read on and off throughout his life, a book that travelled with him to his various residences, and that he read from and recommended to friends. References to the *Travels* in Coleridge's Notebooks and correspondence are scattered over many years, and it is not possible to determine exactly when he first discovered the work, but in all probability it was some time between the years 1793 and the beginning of 1795, a period when Coleridge was reading avidly about America. He and a handful of close and idealistic friends (which included the future Poet Laureate Robert Southey) were fixated with the idea of emigrating to the New World and there forming, in Coleridgean terminology, a 'pantisocratic' (or 'all-governing', i.e. 'governed by all') society, in which they would live a life of communal harmony, passing the days in mild farmwork ('two to three hours a day'), reading, writing, and engaging in stimulating conversation; this dream of a Utopian garden-world of creativity is strongly echoed in 'Kubla Khan'. Although the pantisocratic plan proved ultimately to be short-lived and ill-fated, Coleridge had typically taken it to heart with great earnestness, and had even gone so far as to make an improvident marriage on the premise that spouses would be required by all pantisocrats to ensure the domestic stability of the commune.

The pantisocrats eventually determined that the Susequehanna territory of Pennsylvania was the most suitable for their purposes, but it is difficult to believe that Coleridge, who characteristically cast a wide net when researching a new subject, would not have come across Bartram's well-known book at this time; and if he did, how could his restless imagination, in this Utopian quest, not have fallen prey to its spell and not have envisaged the possibility of residing in this southern Eden?

Coleridge's Notebook for the year 1797 contains two lengthy passages about alligators from Bartram's *Travels*, an entry describing the tears of his son Hartley after a fall, and these following enigmatic lines:

> – some wilderness-plot, green & fountainous & unviolated by Man.

The first of the two long passages describes an 'old Champion' alligator; the second is a page-long account of Florida's exotic flora and fauna – the 'milkwhite fragrant blossoms' of the Gordonia lasianthus, which grows by ponds and rivers, and the 'Snake-bird' with its slender long neck and glossy feathers. Several entries later, there is another, final reference to Bartram, in this case to his fanciful description of the 'Life of the Siminole' as being one of never-ending sport and play. The sources of these disjointed references are to be found between pages 127 and 221 of the *Travels*, and thus indicate known parameters of Coleridge's reading at this time.

The enigmatic reference to the 'wilderness-plot, green and fountainous' recurs in a letter Coleridge wrote to his brother not long afterwards in the following interesting context:

> Laudanam gave me repose, not sleep; but you, I believe, know how divine that repose is, what a spot of enchantment, a green spot of fountain and flowers and trees in the very heart of a waste of sands!

Now, on page 157 of the *Travels*, flanked, as Lowes reminds us, 'by our old friends the crocodiles and snake-birds', is this enticing passage, in which is echoed the common language of Coleridge's letter and the 'wilderness-plot' Notebook entry:

> I was however induced to . . . touch at the inchanting little Isle of Palms. This delightful spot, planted by nature, is almost an entire grove of Palms . . . blessed unviolated spot of earth! rising from the limpid waters of the lake; its fragrant groves and blooming lawns invested and protected by encircling ranks of the Yucca gloriosa; a fascinating atmosphere surrounds this blissful garden; the balmy Lantana, ambrosial Citra, perfumed Crinum, perspiring their mingled odours, wafted through Zanthoxilon groves. I at last broke away from the enchanting spot . . .

The fact that Coleridge associated images of fountains and flowers with laudanum – as we know from his letter – makes it all the more likely that as he slipped into the historic laudanum dream that presaged 'Kubla Khan', his mind had already drifted into Bartram's landscape. For it is here on the little Isle of Palms that one finds the chief inspiration for Xanadu's encircled gardens, blossoming with many an incense-bearing tree, and with its forests enfolding sunny spots of greenery.

Bartram's second contribution is yet more central to the poem. On pages 230–31 of the *Travels* there occurs a singularly lyrical and captivating description of 'the admirable Manate Spring'. Although it lies outside the parameters of Coleridge's reading of Bartram documented by the Notebook, it does so by only nine pages. The proof is in the text, which affords a taste of Bartram's narrative at its most inimitably lush:

> we now ascended the crystal stream, the current swift, we entered the grand fountain, the expansive circular bason, the source of which arises from under the bases of the high woodland hills, near half encircling it; the ebullition is astonishing, and continual, though its greatest force or fury intermits, regularly, for the space of thirty seconds of time; the waters

appear of a lucid sea green colour, in some measure owing to the reflection of the leaves above; the ebullition is perpendicular upwards, from a vast ragged orifice through a bed of rocks, a great depth below the common surface of the bason, throwing up small particles or pieces of white shells, which subside with the waters, at the moment of intermission, gently settling down round about the orifice, forming a vast funnel; ...

In addition to 'Manate Spring', Bartram offers another candidate for the 'mighty fountain' of 'Kubla Khan'. On page 165, just beyond the Gordonia lasianthus which Coleridge mentioned in his Notebook, Bartram writes:

I seated myself upon a swelling green knoll, at the head of the crystal bason ... in front, just under my feet was the inchanting and amazing crystal fountain, which incessantly threw up, from dark, rocky caverns below, tons of water every minute, forming a bason ... a creek of four or five feet depth of water, and near twenty yards over, which meanders six miles through green meadows, pouring its limpid waters into the great Lake George ... About twenty yards from the upper edge of the bason ... is a continual and amazing ebullition, where the waters are thrown up in such abundance and amazing force, as to jet and swell up two or three feet above the common surface: white sand and small particles of shells are thrown up with the waters ...

It does not take much imagination to see how the graphic lines of these two passages were combined into the dream cadence of 'Kubla Khan':

... And from this chasm, with ceaseless turmoil seething,
As if this earth in fast thick pants were breathing,
A mighty fountain momently was forced:
Amid whose swift half-intermitted bursts
Huge fragments vaulted like rebounding hail,
Or chaffy grain beneath the thresher's flail:

And 'mid these dancing rocks at once and ever
It flung up momently the sacred river.
Five miles meandering with a mazy motion
Through wood and dale the sacred river ran,
Then reached the caverns measureless to man,
And sank in tumult to a lifeless ocean . . .

From Bartram's itinerary we know that the little Isle of Palms and mighty fountain were to be found in the same corner of the Florida landscape: the mighty fountain is both Manatee Springs, some twenty miles west of Gainesville, and Salt Springs, set squarely in the Ocala National Forest; the Isle of Palms lies off Rocky Point on the northwest shore of Lake George and the meandering sacred river is Salt Springs Run, which winds five miles from the springs down to the great sea of Lake George.

The popular perception of Florida as a place of beaches and holiday sites does not, generally speaking, accommodate the wilder Africanesque features highlighted by Bartram's writings and the *Tarzan* films. The north of Florida, however, is little visited and little known, and is historically, demographically and climactically, as well as scenically, a world apart from the popular central and southern regions. The fact that over eighty per cent of the total population resides in the central and southern two-thirds is in itself telling. While all of Florida is extremely low-lying (on average less than a hundred feet above sea level), what hills exist are in the north. Northern Florida is subtropical (on the same latitude as Egypt), with an average annual temperature of 68 degrees Fahrenheit, compared to 77 degrees in the far south, which means that in addition to the ubiquitous pines, palms and cypresses, the northern forests harbour magnolia, tulip, hickory and sweet-gum trees. The north is mostly rural, and its *mores* are more akin to those of the Old South than to anything found in the aggressively developed, urban central and southern areas, which foster the hot-spots of artificial culture for which Florida is best known, such as Disney World and Miami Beach.

When telling people about Tallahassee, I have often described the city and its outskirts as seen from the air – its rolling hills and dense forests, then, closer to the airport itself, the thin rivers and dark lakes that alone break through the trees; and always, when peering out of the plane window myself, on the verge of return, I am somewhat taken aback to see that the land in fact appears to be exactly as it is elsewhere in Florida – board-flat. From the air the tree-cover appears extensive, but seems to be composed mostly of new pines, and does not really warrant the term 'forest'. The weather was dull throughout this particular trip to the landmarks of Xanadu, which may have accounted for the lacklustre appearance of the greenery and the muddy streams that wound through it as we approached for landing. In the few cleared plots one could see where grass had worn away to reveal an insubstantial sandy substrata. A few of these clearings were for trailer parks, which I did not remember having seen before.

I had chosen my mother as guide for the journey, the sites in question lying just outside Gainesville, and thus in territory that she knew from her pioneering days. We left Tallahassee on another dull June day, taking Florida Route 27 south to Gainesville through drab roadside scenery of monotonous pine plantations and low scrubland, tenuously settled by solitary shacks and small ramshackle communities. Intriguing dirt trails lead off from the main road into forest, but as few people have cause to follow them, the overwhelming common impression must be of roughly cleared land and hastily built convenience stores and houses. Occasionally these are built ranch-style in harsh red brick, but more usually in sloping, weathered wood. Sometimes a handsome wooden house set picturesquely under live-oaks of inordinate size and age will indicate a family place of several generations, but ordinarily the buildings one passes give the appearance of having been constructed from the necessity or inspiration of the moment, and never intended to do more than serve their present occupants.

Manatee Springs lies off the east bank of the Suwannee River, some two hundred miles down its two-hundred-and-fifty-mile course from the Okefenokee Swamp to the Gulf of Mexico. Like most of Florida's springs of greater magnitude, it is now enshrined within the confines of a state park, and while naturally situated in dense forest, its south bank has been converted to a discreet picnic area, set in kempt grounds, and only studded with pine trees. The north shore of the spring basin recedes between cypress knees that rise like the knuckles of a giant hand from the water, behind which a scanty beach retreats into an unmolested ash and gum-tree forest. The opposite bank, by contrast, is reinforced by a retaining wall to which a ladder is affixed, providing easy access to the water. In a similar gesture of thoughtfulness, an elaborate wooden boardwalk directs the visitor around the southern shore, which is also overlooked by a boathouse and refreshment stand, built of 'natural' wood and therefore supposedly unobtrusive. Close to the spring itself a plaque surmounts the wooden railing of the boardwalk, engraved with Bartram's captivating description of its 'astonishing and continual' ebullition; and thus the modern tourist is advised that he is following in the footsteps of an earlier traveller who beheld the scene in its former sparkling glory.

By way of the strategic ladder, I lowered myself into the chill water, which like that of all of Florida's springs hovers somewhere between 68 and 72 degrees Fahrenheit. While Bartram had suggested that the 'sea green' colour of the spring was a reflection of the overhanging greenery, the clear, dark water that I entered seemed to be coloured by the springs' depths. The trees were in any case changing colour: the tips of the feathery cypress leaves were now, as if it were autumn, a blur of gold, yellowy-green and red. Under the water close to the eastern shore, a clump of trees had apparently fallen headlong, and now lay like moss-covered monuments to be dredged up at a later date – cannons from a sunken ship. A deep hole fell away from them below a ledge of jutting rock, which marked the entrance to an underwater channel leading to an adjacent pool. A few small fish wound peaceably around the long grass tendrils that stretched towards the exit channel to the south, rooted in a long swathe of displaced sand. This movement, I soon discovered, was caused by the spring boil, the specific point whence the underwater stream breaks with hidden force into the pool. Swimming towards it underwater, I was suddenly punched backwards into a small and murky cloud of fine sand that had been flung up by the boil from the basin floor. This was the mighty fountain, whose force over two hundred years ago had shown itself to Bartram above the surface of the spring. The ground-water pressure that once produced the fountain has dwindled over the centuries as land was drained and developed, and the water table reduced to meet the needs of human consumption.

Two divers had just emerged from making the journey through the narrow underwater channel linking the springs with the pool that lay a hundred yards or so beyond, a seemingly perfect round hole of impenetrable and sinister darkness set incongruously in the placid picnic grounds behind us. A fine covering of duckweed had absorbed the outer edges of its absolutely opaque water so as to form a kind of fantastic abstract painting. The underwater channel passes through an extensive, 2000-foot-long system of caves, the divers reported, the most renowned of which was dubbed Catfish Hotel. A permanent rope guides the way through the central passage, and the side-channels and attendant caves thus tend to go unexplored. The water had been murky on this run, I was told, but these underwater caverns are said to be very beautiful, being an unexpected reddish-brown. Florida's porous limestone substructure is riddled with such subterranean waterways, which on breaking out into open ground yield the sink-holes, springs and basins that pock the forests: twenty-seven of the nation's nearly eighty major springs are in Florida. The enduring temptation to explore these caverns measureless to man is great and each year extracts its fatalities: two other divers had drowned in the Manatee Springs channel the preceding August.

One of the present divers re-entered the water to retrieve the motorised, lamplit underwater scooter on which he had trundled around in the darkness of the black pool's bottom. His underwater progress could be marked by the intermittent line of slow-breaking bubbles that temporarily disturbed the duckweed. Above him in the picnic grounds, a group of female prisoners on an outing from the local jail had disembarked from their bus and were sullenly taking their places on the wooden picnic benches, while their guards stood and chatted with one of the park officials.

The outflowing of the springs was channelled down a corridor of trees about a quarter of a mile long into the Suwannee River, which from this vantage point appeared dark and placid. This vista at least, one could happily imagine, had changed very little since Bartram's time. Behind me, two families, out-of-state tourists, judging from their accents and comments, approached the springs with their myriad children. The little boys stood in a wary line along the spring edge, commenting on the weed and fish and depth of the water. Their careful reverence highlighted what I felt myself to be missing; namely, a sensibility capable of elevating the scene above the merely picturesque to something worthy of its romantic pedigree.

In a passage that could well serve as a definition of the Romantic point of view, Coleridge praised Wordsworth for his gift 'of spreading the tone, the *atmosphere* ... of the ideal world around forms, incidents, and situations of which, for the common view, custom had bedimmed all the lustre, had dried up the sparkle and the dewdrops'. The landscape of 'Kubla Khan' (as of Bartram's *Travels*) is exclusive, and the sense the poem gives of uncommon access to an unaccustomed realm is part of its powerful attraction. Here in the state park, however, little meaningful distinction could be drawn between common and poetic views of this landmark of Xanadu; a visitor could not but be aware of the countless beholdings of this same scene by others, of the manifold layers of common perceptions that had been laid upon it. As Bartram and Coleridge had proved, landscape is less memorably described than it is interpreted; and if one can romanticise a raw setting by point of view alone, one can, surely, similarly domesticate it.

'Many geographical myths have a poetical tradition before becoming a generally accepted belief promoting voyages and discoveries.' The author of this passage was not referring to the legend of Xanadu, but to that of the Fountain of Youth, which had been one of the primary lures (the other being gold) that led Ponce de León, the 'discoverer' of Florida, to the peninsula in the first place. The legend derived from fanciful accounts of an Earthly Paradise somewhere 'extra Gangem', in which the Fountain was said to lie. According to medieval traditions, the Fountain of Youth burst forth in a forest of evergreen trees set in a blooming landscape that was fanned by breezes bearing the sweet perfume of flowers. The faith in these poetic legends was great enough to convince explorer after explorer, from Columbus onwards, in the face of compelling scientific evidence to the contrary, that in the tropical landscape of the New World they had found the fabled land beyond the Ganges; testimony, as one historian has written, 'to the influence of legendary geography over actual experience'.

The early explorers apart, Florida has historically attracted people on romantic quests. Beginning in the 1820s, when the introduction of steam riverboats made the waterways accessible to travellers, invalids made their way down south, dreaming of finding health in Florida's legendary sunshine. A century later, there began the land speculation boom in the wake of the mass migration of resort-seekers and retirees from the cold northern and midwestern states, the first of multitudes to fall prey to the Utopian dream of a haven of rest, and perhaps, too, of some miracle of rejuvenation akin to the Fountain of Youth. John Muir, the patriarch of American wilderness preservation, wrote in his diary, on first entering Florida in his tramp across the country, that:

> In visiting Florida in dreams, of either day or night, I always came suddenly on a close forest of trees, every one in flower, and bent down and entangled to network by luxuriant, bright-blooming vines, and over all a flood of bright sunlight.

The organised marketing of this apparently perennial dream of youth, sun, health and flowers constitutes Florida's modern tourist industry, which caters to thirty million people a year. Nearly half of Florida's 58,500-square-mile area is consigned to beaches, forests and federal and state parks, the latter managed, according to a tourist brochure I came across, 'to appear as they did when the first Europeans arrived ... Florida's state parks fulfil an important purpose as representative examples of "Original Natural Florida".'

Original Natural Florida was, in fact, inhabited, before the coming of the Europeans, by Indians, who are believed to have migrated down into the state as much as ten thousand years ago. The first inhabitants were primarily hunters, gatherers and fishers and, from around 500 BC, farmers. By the mid-eighteenth century, these Florida peoples had been driven into virtual extinction by European and Creek interference, through the medium of their alien diseases, wars, slave raids and religious persecutions.

In 1565, the Spanish established the mission of St Augustine on the northeastern coast of Florida, the first permanent European settlement in the New World. Fever, the hostility of the local inhabitants and the wildness of the land and weather, however, prohibited development, apart from a few other doomed mission and military stations along the coast and coastal rivers. In 1763, England and Spain exchanged Havana and Florida, and the next twenty years saw a period of emigration from England to the new possession; it was during this brief period of British occupation that Bartram made his travels. In 1779, Spain declared war against Britain, and West Florida was subsequently captured for his country by the Spanish governor of New Orleans. Four years later, under the terms of the Treaty of Paris, Florida was formally handed back to Spain. After many vicissitudes of possession and fortune, in 1819, East and West Florida were ceded by Spain to the United States.

In 1817, the first of what would be three Seminole Wars had broken out, ostensibly over the Government's concern to recapture runaway slaves who had settled among the Seminoles. Although for most Floridians the Seminoles represent 'our' Original Natural Inhabitants, this tribe did not in fact appear on the Florida scene until the late eighteenth century, some two hundred years after the arrival of the Europeans. Descended from the Muskogean-speaking Creek tribes, the Seminoles were breakaway migrants from the Georgia Creeks who were later joined by runaway black and Indian slaves; Florida had acquired the reputation of being a haven for fleeing slaves from 1699, in the time of Spanish possession of the territory, when a Spanish royal decree promised protection to all slaves who reached Florida and converted to Catholicism. The name 'Seminole' is believed to have derived from the Spanish *cimarrón*, meaning 'wild' – the same etymological origin as that of the Maroons of the Caribbean.

That the real issue behind the Seminole conflicts was land became unambiguously apparent in the course of the next two wars, which were fought on and off until 1858. In contention was the territory north of Lake Okeechobee, which had been designated as a Seminole reserve, but had come to be coveted by white settlers, whose fundamental aim was the removal of the Seminoles from Florida. In this they were almost completely successful. Most of the tribe was transported in 1842, at the end of the second of the wars and shortly before Florida was awarded statehood, to the Creek reservation in what is now Oklahoma. Only a handful remained in Florida, and while in Bartram's time the Seminoles possessed 'a vast territory: all East Florida and the greatest part of West Florida', the present population is estimated to number only one thousand. Virtually no vestiges of their former wide-ranging presence remain, apart from the euphonious names with which they endowed their towns and lakes and rivers.

At the time when civil government was imposed in 1822, the Florida territory constituted a vast expanse of unexplored wilderness and a 1200-mile coastline that had never been properly surveyed. A few years later, only a modest stretch of road had been built, and only sixty-three miles of rail laid. Until the establishment of rail networks in the late nineteenth century, transportation had to rely upon the extensive waterways of this wild and difficult land. In northern Florida, few rivers offered more intriguing possibilities than that called by the Indians Welaka, later to be renamed the St Johns. Although affording the primary route of William Bartram's famous travels, its source and entire course were not known at the time of his journey. A prospectus written by the explorer Le Conte nearly fifty years after Bartram, in 1821, for an expedition up the river eloquently conveys the challenge of discovery. In language reminiscent of the earliest explorers of other unknown continents, it cites as its main goal the desire 'to explore the St Johns river to its source, through a country utterly unknown, and it is believed as yet untrodden by the foot of a European'.

Welaka in Seminole means 'river of lakes', a name indicating that the precursors of the Europeans at least had understood the essential nature of the uncharted river which, in its three-hundred-mile course from the St Johns Marsh in southeast Florida to the Atlantic, opens out periodically so as to form a chain of lakes. The beauty of this river, even in eyes less forgiving than Bartram's, was legendary. An army soldier travelling this way in the course of duty during the early years of the Second Seminole War – a man whose official duties, surely, precluded the naïve ebullience of Bartram's outlook – eulogised the river in a manner entirely befitting his more effusive predecessor: 'Never shall I forget my sensations at that rare and beauteous sight!' he exclaims of his entry to the river.

> A succession of glorious scenery was constantly presented to the sight, as we rapidly stemmed the St Johns; whose banks, now receding, now approximating so as merely to admit our boat between them, were bright in loveliness on either side with every species of tree and shrub. From orange groves, whose golden fruit and snowy blossom stood in beautiful contrast to their dark foliage, we'd pass on to long rows of tall and slim palmettoes; their graceful trunks shooting up along the river banks for miles. Then a change would come over the beauty of the scenery; and in place of orange and palm trees, would appear the spreading oak, the bay, the beautiful cedar, and stately magnolia; their pendant branches casting mysterious shadows on the St Johns ...

Salt Springs lies off the western shore of Lake George which, at eleven miles in length, is the largest of the chain of lakes opening off the St Johns river. The history of the springs site reflects much of the larger history of Florida as a whole. In the early seventeenth century, rights to it and to the outflowing Salt Springs Run were granted by the King of Spain to the Hernandez family, Portuguese settlers in the area with whom he was on friendly terms. The land remained, undeveloped, in their possession until the late 1800s, when an entrepreneur from Georgia laid claim to the more or less forgotten grant, seeing in the Run in particular a possibility for an inland shipping route to the Jacksonville depots. In 1908, the scrub forest surrounding the springs was made a National Forest, although – being in the backwoods as it was – the spring remained undiscovered by tourists. In the 1920s the Hernandez land grant was sold by the Georgian entrepreneur to a local family, who in turn sold the bulk of it outright to the Federal Government in 1979, for twelve million dollars. The story of this lengthy and complicated transaction is part of local lore, and every resident of the area contests the legality of one detail or another. No one in this tiny, self-contained settlement, however, accepts the fact that the springs in which they grew up swimming and fishing now belongs to the US Federal Government.

Bass'n, Etc. Fishing Guide Service, located on the edge of Highway 19 in the Salt Springs township, was, I had been told, the best place from which to hire a boat. Although I had been given specific and accurate directions, the town came and went so quickly that we had passed through it before we started to look for landmarks. Backtracking, we soon found it among the few roadside buildings, a small red and white wooden lean-to, selling fishing gear and tackle, and otherwise catering to the limited needs of its community.

Layman Lane, our guide-to-be, was a good ol' boy of sorts, but tamed to some extent by his love for his wife Glenda, a diminutive, fiery woman and one of the descendants of the legendary Portuguese Hernandez family. We were, we were made to understand, on her family's property.

Hitching his boat expertly to his truck, Layman led the way off the main road and down a sandy lane overshadowed by moss-draped oaks towards the water. Here, well hidden behind the drab scrubland and the make-do buildings lay, largely undisturbed, the land that Bartram had rhapsodised and the inspiration of poets. The basin of the springs proper lay ringed with massive oaks to the left, while the boat pier and the adjacent boathouse faced directly on the Run. An aloof egret standing rooted in the screen of reeds watched our departure in the boat. The springs were empty, and the lone caretaker of the boathouse appeared to be the only other person around.

The day which had begun dull had not brightened and the overcast water was grey and clear and, according to Layman, waving a hand at a band of parasite bulrushes by way of illustration, not doing well, although the culprit, unexpectedly, was in this case not Man, but Nature. A constant easterly wind prohibits the outflow of the Run's waters, and their exit thus pent up at the Run-mouth allows waves of Lake George's brackish tannin-tinged water to surge in. Layman Lane could remember when the bullrushes had not been there and when the water had been truly pristine. He had come here from the Blue Ridge Mountains of Tennessee in 1956, looking for work. In season, he is a fishing guide; off-season, he fishes for himself in the Run, which teems with bass and mullet, and in favourite cypress swamps nearby.

The crowns of small palm clusters showed their heads above the forest of the Run's narrow shores, and the foliage was brightened here and there by cascading clumps of white water violets. Cranes and egrets stood immovable in the reeds, an unutterable weight of silence contained in their unbudging silhouettes. The steady, vandal easterly flickered up the pale undersides of the leaves of the higher trees, but made little dent in the massive luxuriance of the lower foliage. On the left shore, a shell midden stood out against the greenery, a casual token of the generations of Indian possession of this land.

At the entrance of Lake George two important landmarks came into view: a rocky point on the left bank, mentioned by Bartram, and the great shaggy wedge of Drayton's Island, now privately owned. Between these two, a low-water warning marker was the only feature to break the tea-coloured water and, on cautiously approaching, one could see the V of a low-water current catching the sand. This marker, embedded in a hidden protrusion, stands where one would expect to find the little Isle of Palms, that blessed, unviolated spot of earth and its incense-bearing trees. Perhaps accumulated river silt has incorporated it into the river delta, or perhaps two hundred years of storm and erosion have washed it away, down into the dark brown sun-defying sea of Lake George.

With a diameter of six miles at this point, the lake's own shores are distant and indistinct, offering little to view apart from a low, rough line on the horizon. From the vantage point of the Run-mouth, the near shore, too, was unremarkable, a high sand bar covered with saw-grass and palmettos. But on nearby Drayton's Island, one could glean some idea of what the little Isle of Palms might have looked like. The island is covered with two thousand acres of forest, which from the tossing boat appeared unviolated, although Layman reported that there had been a great fire here some years ago. Close to the water's edge, so as to benefit from its warm currents, a striking grove of palms claims the shoreline, their shafts and crowns the only features of distinction for miles around to make any impression between the dark water and the dull sky. The flora harboured on the island, as everywhere in the area, however, has been sadly diminished since Bartram's time: a severe freeze that descended in February of 1835 killed off the fabled centuries' old orange groves whose scent wafting over the river had been admired even by toughened conquistadores.

Just beyond the delta of the river-mouth, heading back into the Run, we passed an old man contentedly fishing in a moored boat.

'He's a retired fisherman,' Layman informed us approvingly. It was by now early evening, and the shore vegetation had begun to blur into a featureless bank of shadows. Two wildcats spat and thrashed from somewhere in the forest, and an osprey, perhaps disturbed by their antics, shot out of the treetops. The same sombre sand-mound crane stood at stiff attention on an overhead branch framed with Spanish moss and, back at the entrance to the springs, the same spotless egret gleamed out from the dark reeds he was guarding.

The small boathouse was being closed up as we disembarked, but there was time enough to visit the shop and to read the literature taped to its walls, odds and ends relating to the history of the springs. A newspaper cutting detailing an alligator attack some years back was displayed, with, one sensed, some pride, and as a kind of

warning to the northern sun-bunnies who make their way here
during winter and spring vacations that this is a place to be taken
seriously. Tourism did not come to Salt Springs until the 1960s,
when Highway S-19 opened up the Ocala National Forest. The lack
of motels and tourist conveniences bespeaks the fact that visitors are
only grudgingly received, and most have to make do with camp-sites.
One has to have lived here a long time to count as more than a
newcomer.

Salt Springs is a circular basin measuring some one hundred
feet in diameter, set in a grove of ancient, twisted-rooted oaks.
The springs take their name from the mild salty flavour of the
water, attributed to trace minerals and saline residues retained,
from an era when this place was under the sea, in the limestone
through which it filters. As far back as Indian times, medicinal
value was attributed to the water, and in modern times as well the
site is still used for 'healing'. It is claimed by some that Salt
Springs, with its preservative salts and minerals, is the Fountain of
Youth sought by Ponce de León – but of what spring in Florida is
this not said?

Five boils barely rippled the surface of the basin; but even today,
when the ground water has been raised by a period of sustained rain,
these jets have been seen to spurt as high as four inches above the
water. In Bartram's time, the boils had formed a spectacular fountain,
flumes of water erupting from the basin floor with force enough to
carry along fragments of sand and shell. Now, through the crystal
water, I could see that the sandy floor was clouded and disturbed
around the hidden boils.

Glenda Lane, dispossessed inheritor of the springs, had come over
to show us around while her husband cranked the boat back on to its
trailer. It was by now dark, and the concrete retaining walls and
guardrails with which National Park status has improved the springs
could happily be overlooked. Mrs Lane was not concerned whether
the park was officially open or closed.

'The US Federal Government will charge you one dollar and fifty
cents for the privilege of crossing this strip of grass,' she said with
unconcealed contempt. No one at the ticket booth had attempted to

extract an admission fee from us, but then we were with Glenda Lane.

'The springs were willed to the people of Florida by Mr Ray,' she informed us, revealing yet another complication – unsubstantiated as it turned out – in the history of the springs' ownership. 'The US Federal Government only owns the grass. If you swim in from the Run, there is nothing they can do.' Glenda Lane was among the many local people who repeatedly came out at night to tear down the wire fence the US Federal Government had attempted to erect around the area shortly after it had acquired the property. While not romantically inclined, the people of Salt Springs, Florida, had matter-of-factly recognised the beauty of this site, and it was only with bitterness and resistance that they surrendered their blessed, unviolated spot of earth.

'The imagination,' Coleridge wrote, 'I hold to be the living power and prime agent of all human perception.' I was, at this journey's end, forced to recognise that the picture of Florida I had often offered – to myself as well as others – had been, like Bartram's account, highly edited and selective. While I always recalled the woods and flowers, the wild thunderstorms and savage sunsets, I had tended to forget the shopping malls, or that the oak-canopied roads of Tallahassee are often looped with ungainly telephone cables. The trick was somehow to maintain, as Coleridge admonished, 'the fine balance of truth in observing with the imaginative faculty in modifying the objects observed'.

However, the elusive images of Xanadu could not, on this particular journey, be apprehended by truthful observation of the places that inspired them – the vanished little Isle of Palms and the exhausted, domesticated fountains. The one place where they might reside I did not visit, being unwilling to risk disturbing remembered images by an actual journey to Wakulla. Truthful observation might prove me wrong; but I believe it was there, years ago, that I saw the wilderness-plot, green and fountainous, of Coleridge's imagination.

In some sense, then, the Florida journey was one I had no need to make – like Coleridge, I could have conjured what I sought without straying far from home. But the other objects of my quest lay far afield and on unfamiliar territory.

THE

CAVE

OF

ICE

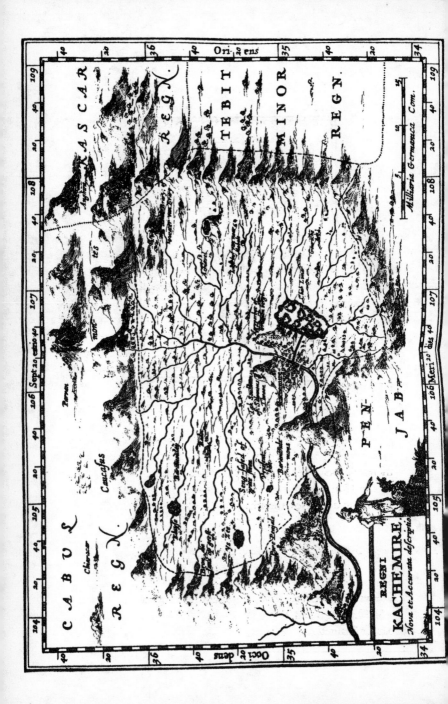

The Cave of Ice

One of Coleridge's most endlessly projected works was a collection of six poems to be entitled *Hymns to the Sun, the Moon, and the Elements*. This masterwork was outlined, discussed among friends, researched extensively – but never begun. Nevertheless, his incessant quest after material for his *opus* led him down many an interesting byway, nor was it to prove entirely fruitless – the results of his researches ended up in large part in *The Ancient Mariner*.

Two pages after the long passages copied from Bartram's *Travels*, the following consecutive entries – most pertaining to Kashmir – appear in the 1797 Notebook:

Hymns Moon

In a cave in the mountains of Cashmere an Image of Ice, which makes its appearance thus – two days before the new *moon* there appears a bubble of Ice which increases in size every day till the 15th day, at which it is an ell or more in height: then as the moon decreases, the Image does also till it vanishes.

Read the whole 107th page of Maurice's Indostan.

Sun

Hymns – Remember to look at Quintius Curtius
– lib. 3. Cap. 3 and 4.
Major Rennell

The first passage quoted is from a work entitled *The History of Hindostan*, written by the Reverend Thomas Maurice and published in 1795. This is an ambitious, two-volume undertaking to expound not only the arts, sciences and, above all, religions of India, but to relate them to 'the History of the Other Great Empires of Asia, during the Most Ancient Periods of the World'. Crammed as it is with erudite and arcane mythology and history, it was a work after Coleridge's own heart. The excerpted passage in full reads as follows:

> In a cave of the same mountainous subah a very singular phaenomenon is said, in the Ayeen Akbery, at certain periods to make its appearance. Though to the last degree absurd and incredible, the relation will yet illustrate the present subject, and what will hereafter occur concerning their computation of time by the bright and dark appearance of the moon's orb. In this cave, says Abul Fazil, is sometimes to be seen an image of ice, called AMERNAUT, which is holden in great veneration. This image makes its appearance after the following manner:

There follows the passage noted by Coleridge.

On the page preceding this, Maurice cites the Roman historian Quintus Curtius, giving a book and chapter reference that Coleridge had simply jotted down (misspelling his name) to confirm first-hand, as was his habit, at a later date. The abbreviated reference to Major James Rennell's work, *Memoir of a Map of Hindoostan: or the Mogul's Empire*, however, is more intriguing. Maurice, in the 'Preliminary Chapter' to his history, directs his 'reader's attention to the intelligent Memoir, and very accurate map of Hindostan, presented to the world by Major Rennell'. In the section on 'Cashmere', the region wherein was said to lie the cave of ice that had clearly captured Coleridge's imagination, Major Rennell breaks momentarily away from his characteristic dry tone and offers the following memorable tribute:

> The valley or country of Cashmere, is celebrated throughout upper Asia for its romantic beauties, for the fertility of its soil,

and for the temperature of its atmosphere ... it is an elevated and extensive valley, surrounded by steep mountains, that tower above the regions of snow; ... The author of the Ayin Acbaree dwells with rapture on the beauties of Cashmere ... [the] emperors of Hindoostan visited it also, and seemed to forget the cares of government, during their residence in *the happy valley* ... only light showers fall there: these, however, are in abundance enough to feed some thousands of cascades, which are precipitated into the valley, from every part of the stupendous and romantic bulwark that encircles it ... In a word, the whole scenery is beautifully picturesque ... All Cashmere is holy land; and miraculous fountains abound.

A final literary reference needs to be mentioned, although Coleridge does not name it in his Notebook. In the first paragraph of his dissertation on 'Cashmere', Major Rennell cites François Bernier, a French physician who in the seventeenth century had travelled extensively in the valley while in the service of the Mogul king, as being 'the most instructive of all Indian travellers'. It is difficult to believe that Coleridge, who was clearly hot on the Kashmiri trail, would have overlooked this compelling citation. That he did in fact follow up this reference appears more likely when one considers what Bernier has to say in his chapter entitled 'Journey to Kachemire':

The most beautiful of all these gardens is one belonging to the King, called *Chah-limar*. The entrance from the lake is through a spacious canal ... It leads to a large summer-house placed in the middle of the garden. A second canal, still finer than the first, then conducts you to another summer-house, at the end of the garden ... In the middle is a long row of fountains, fifteen paces asunder ... The summer-houses are placed in the midst of the canal, consequently surrounded by water ... They are built in the form of a dome ...

Returning from *Send-brary*, I turned a little from the high road for the sake of visiting *Achiavel*, a house formerly of the Kings of

Kachemire, and now of the *Great Mogol*. What principally constitutes the beauty of this place is a fountain ... The spring
gushes out of the earth with violence, as if it issued from the
bottom of some well, and the water is so abundant that it ought
rather to be called a river than a fountain ... The garden is very
handsome, laid out in regular walks, and full of fruit trees –
apple, pear, plum, apricot, and cherry.

Maurice, we know, to quote Lowes, 'beyond peradventure'
Coleridge had read; Major Rennell we know he intended to read,
and more likely than not did so: Bernier he may well have read. In the
collected writings of these authors one may discern the romantic
chasm, the holy place, the dome, echoes of the mighty fountain
and – found in no other source – the cave of ice of Xanadu. The
Notebook, therefore, shaped the itinerary for my third journey
around three places in Kashmir: the Shalimar Gardens outside
modern Srinagar: the Achabal Gardens lying just off the main road to
the hill station of Pahalgam: and the Amarnath Cave situated at some
thirteen thousand feet in the foothills of the Himalayas.

Two days before my departure, I went to the Indian Consulate to
pick up visas.

'You must step upstairs, into the main Embassy, I'm afraid,' said
the pleasantly smiling woman behind the counter grille. 'They must
just want to talk to you,' she added, when with mild alarm I queried
why I alone of the queuing crowd had been thus singled out.

Upstairs, I was shown into the office of a sombre-looking man,
who sat regarding me in silence for a few minutes, before clasping his
hands and leaning forward to address me.

'You cannot go to Kashmir. You know we are having troubles
there.' I knew very well. It was the summer of 1991 and Kashmir
was – as it still is – embroiled in a radical secessionist movement:
hundreds of thousands of Indian government troops, or security
forces as they are officially called, have been sent to the region to fight
the guerrillas and to guard India's border with Pakistan. Only a few
months beforehand, rebels had kidnapped some Israeli tourists who

had been staying on a houseboat on one of the lakes. The captives had been marched out into the darkness at gunpoint – where they had eventually overpowered their guards and escaped. I was, therefore, circumspect about travelling to Kashmir – but also determined to do everything up to a reasonable point to get there. My plan was to get at least to Delhi, from where I felt the situation could be assessed more reliably. So great had been my concern to be 'sensible' about embarking on this enterprise that in a spirit of complete responsibility I had, perhaps foolishly – certainly needlessly – entered Kashmir on my visa application, which requested a list of the places in India that I intended to visit.

'You cannot go to Kashmir.' This statement was repeated intermittently throughout the interview by the gentleman whose specific title I never learned. When it emerged that I wanted to go hiking in the mountains – the Amarnath Cave being several days' journey by foot away from the nearest hill station – I was gently but firmly instructed to take my walk elsewhere. Downstairs again, I collected our passports with their visas, but was also handed a packet of leaflets expounding the rugged beauty of Himachal Pradesh.

George, my travelling companion in Mongolia, and I arrived in Delhi in early August, and what should have been the relatively cooler rainy season. The monsoon had not come, however, and the city was encased in a wadding of stolid, begrimed air. As dual nationals, we had two important visits to make.

'I cannot emphasise strongly enough that officially I have to warn you not to go to Kashmir,' said Her Majesty's Consul. 'The principal danger is of being caught in crossfire. We cannot be responsible for you.'

'He said *officially* he had to warn us,' I said to George afterwards. '*Privately*, he may have thought very differently.' Distressingly, the terse directive we received from the American Embassy conveyed the same message: 'Due to recent terrorist activity in the Kashmir portion of the state of Jammu and Kashmir, Americans should defer travel to the valley of Kashmir until further notice.'

Although we both agreed that the State Department characteristically tended to be over-cautious, my spirits had by now been somewhat dampened. There was, however, one course of action available to us that would reconcile my desire to be sensible with my determination to see the cave of ice. The image of Amarnath which, as Coleridge had read, was 'holden in great veneration' is to this day still very much an object of religious reverence. In the years before the recent political troubles, the Amarnath pilgrimage annually drew as many as thirty thousand devout Hindus to the mountains of Kashmir. As in Coleridge's time, it is believed that the 'image' in the cave of ice waxes and wanes in size in accordance with the phases of the moon. The most propitious time to approach the holy site is during the full moon of the Hindu month of *Shravan*, which corresponds with July or August of the Gregorian calender. Due to the troubles, the pilgrimage had been suspended for the two previous years – an unprecedented break in a centuries' old tradition. But, according to the Kashmir Tourist Office in Delhi, the pilgrimage, or *yatra*, was to be reinstated this year under heavy armed guard. Clearly, the safest – not to mention the most auspicious – way to see the cave of ice was to become *yatris* of Lord Shiva.

Politically speaking, Kashmir is the northern region of the northernmost Indian state of Jammu and Kashmir, which lies between the Punjab plains and the Himalayas. Popularly speaking, it tends to refer specifically to the Vale of Kashmir, a lush and abundant valley in the northwest of the state, contained by the spurs of two great chains of the Himalayas. Measuring some eighty-five by twenty miles in length and breadth, the valley is the basin of an ancient lake, sheltered by mountainous boundaries that stand as high as sixteen thousand feet.

The troubled political history of the state is reflected by its three borders: that to the north and east is shared with China, which has since 1962 illegally occupied a segment of Ladakh, one of the regions of Jammu and Kashmir: that to the northwest is shared with Pakistan, which contends that Kashmir should be in its possession: and that to the south is shared with two Indian states, one of which, Punjab, is embroiled in a secessionist movement of its own.

Prior to 1947, the year in which the departing British raj divided the subcontinent into India and Pakistan, Kashmir had been an independent princely state, enjoying virtual autonomy from the rest of India under the government of the Kashmiri Maharajah. The establishment of the two newly independent nations, however, put pressure on the Maharajah to declare allegiance to one state or the other. While he delayed coming to a decision, a rebellion of his predominantly Muslim subjects, who were in favour of a union with Pakistan, abetted by an invasion of Pathan tribesmen, prompted the intervention of Indian forces. It was India's rescue of the beleaguered Maharajah that determined the fate of the principate as an Indian possession, a claim that continues to be contested by Islamabad. Border skirmishes have plagued Kashmir since its annexation and on two occasions, in 1965 and 1971, have escalated into wars, both of which eventually ended to India's advantage. A United Nations mandate issued in 1949, that the state's allegiance with either India or Pakistan be determined by a plebiscite, has never been honoured. The ongoing antagonism is not purely territorial: of tantamount importance is the fact that Kashmir is a principally Muslim state within a principally Hindu nation.

Since 1990, the situation in Kashmir has progressively worsened, and continues to hover restlessly somewhere between what can euphemistically be termed 'political unrest' and outright war. According to local authorities, as many as one hundred and twenty different guerrilla factions are involved in the uprising, ranging from those who seek Kashmir's complete liberation and restored independence to those who seek its formal annexation to Pakistan and establishment as a fundamentalist Muslim state. The Indian Government, for its part, contends that the situation has assumed the dangerous proportions it has because the guerrillas are trained and sponsored by an enemy nation – a charge that is substantiated in part by confirmation from a number of reliable outside sources that the Pakistani army's intelligence unit runs training camps for fundamentalist guerrillas. This fact notwithstanding, a number of human rights organisations have reported abusive treatment of Kashmiri civilians by the Indian military and, especially, paramilitary forces – which tends to indicate that the government's hostility is not aimed exclusively at Pakistan. As many as three hundred thousand paramilitary and military troops are now estimated to be more or less permanently stationed in Kashmir.

India clearly fears that the secession of Kashmir would be the beginning of the fragmentation of its multi-ethnic nation, and could only fuel further secessionist rebellions, such as those currently under way in Punjab and Assam. On top of all of these considerations is the fact that the Vale of Kashmir has since time immemorial enjoyed the reputation of being one of the most beautiful places on earth and, up until the last three years, had maintained India's most lucrative tourist industry.

Traditionally the Amarnath pilgrimage has begun with the worship of the holy trident in Srinagar, the capital of Jammu and Kashmir. This year, however, so as to skirt the most troubled areas, the pilgrimage formally commenced in the city of Jammu, and then proceeded directly to Pahalgam, the first official camp of the five-day trek to the cave. The unorthodox departure had led many pilgrims to go ahead to Pahalgam on their own so as to wait for the main processional body, or, like us, to start out from Srinagar.

At Srinagar airport a cordon of soldiers encircled our plane as it landed and greeted the disembarking passengers with pointed rifles. Ours was the only commercial plane on the tarmac, all others belonging to the Indian air force. Inside the terminal building, as obvious foreigners, we were requested to fill in elaborate forms explaining our purpose in coming to Kashmir. The statement that we had come to participate in the pilgrimage raised no eyebrows; doubtless there has been a well-established history of Western enthusiasts partaking of this experience.

Srinagar was in days of peace a fairy-tale city, a small gem of almost Central Asian architecture wound around two lakes of surpassing loveliness, and threaded with cobbled alleys and willow-lined canals. The present city dates back to the first century AD, and has for centuries been a centre of learning: its name in Sanskrit means 'city of knowledge'. Rising nearly six thousand feet above the lowland plains, it has been enjoyed as a summer retreat since at least Mogul times.

The city has managed to retain its charm, disconcertingly, in spite of its essential transformation into a garrison. Sandbagged sentry posts were stationed every hundred yards or so along the airport road and along the main streets of the city. With its narrow alleys and passageways, gable-roofed balconies, its deep, dusky shops over-stuffed with piles of fruit, hookahs and carpets, Srinagar strikes one as being designed explicitly for intrigue, and its policing must be a logistical nightmare. The population of the city is over eight hundred thousand and the pervading atmosphere seemed to be a mixture of business-as-usual bravado and sullenness. To a traveller arriving directly from Delhi, the people are strikingly un-Indian in appearance. The faces one sees are the rather heavy-featured, handsome faces of a mountain people, and their clothing, like their architecture, is more Central Asian than Indian – the women were dressed in baggy pants and chadors, the men in pants and short caftans.

It was advisable for us to stay in a houseboat on one of the lakes immediately to the north of the town, rather than in Srinagar itself – in actual fact, few visitors at any time would choose to stay anywhere else. The season had been dry, and the sentry-lined streets were dusty, the roadside herbage sparse and river-beds brown and silted. Lake Negin, when we reached it, was low, its former waterline showing brownly on its rushes. Whereas the Mogul occupiers of Kashmir left exquisite gardens, the houseboats are the peculiar legacy of the British raj, and were the means by which the British circum-vented the Kashmiri Maharajah's prohibition against their acquiring land in his kingdom, as they did elsewhere in India.

Ineffably romantic in theory, the houseboats are in reality bizarre manifestations of British ideas about what constitutes the exotic – miniature fluvial Xanadus from the nation that invented follies and doilies. The houseboat we eventually acquired was a craft whose every visible surface was so intricately and floridly carved as to be nearly porous. Inside, six good-sized bedrooms were ranked along one long corridor, which opened up towards the bow into a dining room, living room and at the tip of the bow, a canopied porch. The interior too was relentlessly embellished with wood-carvings and filled with heavy furniture and other decorations in keeping with this mercifully unique melding of British and Indian 1930s suburban taste.

From the small porch one could look down the long line of house-boats ranged along the shore, moored, like ours, with their sterns to land, their bows facing out into the water. We had arrived at the lake in the late afternoon, and dusk approached with eerie quiet. The summer nightlife on the lakes of Kashmir had once been famous, and at this time of evening there should have been lights, music and voices reflecting off the darkening water. But there was no sign of any other people at all, and I later learned with some astonishment that we were two of only five houseboat occupants. Lake Negin alone harbours two hundred houseboats, each of which is equipped to accommodate at least half a dozen people – and each of which, just two years earlier, would have been booked to capacity. In the 1980s, more than a million Indian and foreign tourists a year provided Kashmir with its most reliable source of income, and virtually all tourists coming to the vale would spend at least one night in Srinagar.

Looking more closely at the lake scenery, I saw that its abandon-ment was taking a heavy toll. Many of the boats lay at awkward angles in the water, or with their sterns sunk a little too deeply in the shoreline rushes. In some places, empty mooring posts rose senselessly from the water. The surface of the water itself was dimpled by thick weeds that choked the lake and spread like lichen just below its surface. I was to learn the next day that it had been two years since the Government had bothered with the usual annual weed-cutting – there was little justification now for this expense. The opposite, west-ern shore of the lake had already disappeared, its margin blurred with a mass of weed and high grass. To the right of our boat, the shore was lost in a more picturesque manner amid stiff, waxy, pink-tipped lotus blossoms and their enormous circular leaves. The occasional flopping of a fish indicated that the lake was not yet entirely dead.

At sunset, Lake Negin momentarily regained its legendary beauty, with the orb of the sun reflected in brief perfection in its mossy waters. The distant mountains that form the ubiquitous background of all scenes in Kashmir gained colour and presence as dusk came on and claimed the foreground. To the southwest, the remains of

Akbar's hill fortress were reduced to an arrogant silhouette. A variety of birds suddenly put in an appearance: fish eagles, kingfishers and swallows swept past the porch, perched on abandoned mooring posts or on the sagging power-line that stood shakily in the water, or hovered overhead on the lookout for prey, with a flagrant confidence that betrayed the fact that they had dismissed the threat of human presence.

As the sun began to disappear, there flashed across the western sky white streaks of gunfire, accompanied by the stammer of automatic rifles, reduced at this distance to mere firework pops. The reflection of the sun continued to spread across the water, and the birds continued to swoop and sing. At six thirty, the mullah's call to the faithful echoed and resonated around the lake in stereophonic sound, issuing as it did from a number of different mosques. This surreal cacophony – the deep thrum of the mullah's ancient call punctuated by the rattle of gunfire and the fearless chatter of the birds – eventually passed, and an unnerving quiet settled in with the night. Until the mullah's morning call, there was nothing at all to be heard throughout this floating ghost town except the soft, insidious lap of water against the boat.

Kashmir was ruled by Hindu kings from the eighth century until the end of the thirteenth, when the assassination of the reigning monarch by his Muslim vizier marked a change of order. The fortunes of Hindu as well as the less numerous Buddhist subjects over the next century were essentially determined by the temperament of the dictator at the time, and reached an unhappy nadir at the close of the fourteenth century under the notorious Sikander, 'breaker of idols'. Elsewhere in India, an old acquaintance, the Mongols, had appeared upon the scene, under the command of Timur Khan, better known as Tamerlane, to whom Sikander submitted and paid tribute. Mongol invasions continued into the sixteenth century, escalating from border skirmishes to the outright conquest of Delhi in 1525. In 1588, Mogul rule was brought to Kashmir by Akbar the Great, and remained in effective power until the mid-eighteenth century, at which time the valley fell to the hands of the Pathans, the notorious and cruel Afghan lords: thus it was they who held sway at the time Coleridge was reading about the beauties of Kashmir. The Pathans lost the valley in 1819 to the Sikh monarchy of the neighbouring Punjab, who retained their prize until 1846, when it was lost in turn to British forces in the Sikh wars. Initially, under the terms of the Treaty of Lahore, it had been stipulated that tribute should be paid for the state to the British Government, but this demand was later waived as a personal favour to Gulab Singh, Sikh general and also maharajah of the neighbouring principality of Jammu, whose neutrality during the wars and important role in the subsequent peace-making process was rewarded with a grant of independent sovereignty over Kashmir.

Within this sequence of foreign rules, that of the Moguls proved to be one of the most beneficent – Mogul being the term used to refer to the Mongol empire in India. The Mogul emperors were descendants of the Chaghataid khans of Central Asia, who had adopted the Muslim religion. They brought to India in general and to Kashmir in particular their religion, military might, administrative skills and their exquisite aesthetic taste, which in Kashmir was most strikingly apparent in their gardens.

Our word 'paradise' is borrowed from the Persian *paradesh*, the walled gardens that surrounded a palace. The Mogul gardens represent one of the great landscape traditions in the world, a fact that should be unsurprising when one considers the lovingly wrought floral patterns and motifs that abound in all forms of Persian art, its manuscripts, carpets and architecture. This love is also, if less expectedly, revealed in the written memoirs of the Kashmiri Moguls: there is a kind of stunning incongruity in reading of the garden-making and botanical passion of men who also record that they were capable of watching their enemies being flayed alive.

'Kashmir is a garden of eternal spring,' wrote Jahangir, Akbar's youngest son, in his autobiography. 'Its pleasant meads and enchanting cascades are beyond all description. There are running streams and fountains beyond count. Wherever the eye reaches, there are verdure and running water. The red rose, the violet, and the narcissus grow of themselves.'

In addition to their natural gifts, the acquisition of India and Kashmir brought the Moguls into contact with the informal exuberance of the more ancient Hindu temple gardens. Indeed, flowers are an integral part of Hindu worship: flowers and masses of rose petals are brought to temples as offerings, and floral designs are used in religious decorative carvings. A third element, deriving directly from the Moguls' Mongol heritage, was the construction of a tomb within the garden grounds, the idea being that a nobleman could take delight in pleasure gardens during his lifetime, but that after his death they would became the province of priests.

Shalimar Gardens, the first of the two gardens described by Bernier, were only a *shikara* ride away from our houseboat. The gardens, which were laid out in the early seventeenth century, were shaped by two men, Jahangir and his son Shah Jahan, who also gave the world the Taj Mahal. (Surely, one of the most formidable dynastic lines in history is that of Genghis Khan and his descendants, which included Khubilai Khan, Tamerlane, Akbar and Shah Jahan.)

A small, brightly canopied punt, or *shikara*, a kind of Kashmiri gondola, appeared off the stern of our houseboat in the morning to take us to Shalimar. The air was cool at this hour, the water dark with the crinkled tendrils of the runaway moss. Drifting past the deserted houseboats and the reedy shore, we entered a long channel at the northern end of Lake Negin that was overhung with willow trees, and which took us into the far larger Lake Dal. Burnt-brick and wooden shuttered houses lay in the willow shade, and the close air underneath the channel trees was briefly and intriguingly fragrant. At the broad waters of Lake Dal, we passed under a clattering bridge, which was heavily sandbagged at each of its sentry-guarded ends, its traffic moving ponderously through the checkpoints. Drifting between a smoking construction site on the left shore and floating islands of vegetation, we began to cross to the far side of the lake by way of an avenue of lotus lilies that rose, crisp and waxy, to shoulder height and were silver-beaded with water. In open water again, we came upon moored punts from which men and women were harvesting the rich lake sludge for use as fertiliser in their fields. Crouched in the extreme bow-end of her shallow craft, as if weighing anchor, a woman was vigorously uprooting choice lily leaves which would be used as fodder for her cattle.

The buildings of Srinagar came into sight on our left, with the white dome of a riverside mosque gleaming conspicuously. We approached an island on our right, breaking into its mirror-perfect reflection. A broken column, jagged and charred, rose among landscaped trees, and was, we were told by the *shikara* punter, all that remained of a once lovely and popular teahouse: it had been burned as a 'political act', whether by militants or army no one knew. The water and sky were the same teal colour by the time we had ploughed through a last meadow of lotus lilies, and reached the shore.

Once upon a time, one entered the gardens directly from the lake, by way of a canal edged with green turf and shaded by poplars, but a road that is being constructed around Lake Dal prohibits this entrance. The dry canal channel is blocked by construction and piles of sand, and the last mile or so must be travelled by road.

From the moment of entering the wall-enclosed garden, one is compulsively drawn towards the long, shallow canal that forms a central aqueous avenue, and which is fed by a spring arising beyond the far wall. The canal is shaded by majestic and heavy-foliaged chenar trees, a kind of oriental plane tree, and the lawns that spread away on either side are dotted with chenars and towering poplars. Flanking the walkways are beds of flowers that, like the poplars which were brought from Italy, are unexpectedly familiar – roses, bougainvillea, gladioli, roses of Sharon, magnolia, crepe myrtle: somehow, one does not expect to come upon marigolds and sweet william in the pleasure gardens of the Mogul kings. While contemporary accounts, including the memoir of Jahangir, make it possible to identify the kinds of trees and flowers used by the Moguls in other gardens, nothing is known about the specific layout of those at Shalimar.

The greatest achievement of the garden does not in any case lie in these natural phenomena. Its distinctive serenity derives mostly from its man-made features – its proportions, the long ornamental canals, the large rectangular pools, the fountain jets, and Bernier's summer-houses, to which all the canals proceed. While the love of the powerful and often cruel Mogul emperors for their gardens might strike one as paradoxical, this is to overlook an essential ingredient in the make-up of the gardens – that of absolute and utter control of all key elements: water, earth and even light. The serenity of Shalimar does not lie in its prettiness. Rather, it is the assured tranquillity born of power – regal, majestic and unassailable: as with 'Kubla Khan', one sensed a mighty shadow presence behind the scene. The garden's encompassing stone wall is low, in part so as not to obscure completely the view of the distant snow-peaked mountains, in part, one feels, because the peace contained within is so secure as to make a defensive wall unnecessary.

Flowing into the smallest of the rectangular pools is an artificial cascade that is presided over by the first of the summerhouses and a black marble slab that served as the emperor's throne. Behind the throne room, the pool narrows, then opens again into an even larger pool. Here, set in a broad square of water, is the garden's centrepiece, an imposing pavilion of black marble. A three-tiered gabled roof surmounts each building; but originally, they had been domed.

It was the vista up and down from the black pavilion that had so captivated Bernier when he described 'the most admirable of all these Gardens', with its painted pleasure houses and its jetting fountains of water. The decorated ceilings, architraves and columns that one sees today were painted, somewhat heavy-handedly, in the mid-nineteenth century; the pools and canals are filled with water, but also with dead leaves, which, downstream, a woman was vainly trying to whisk away with a bracken broom. A sentimental travelogue written in the early 1920s describes the 'terraced pools separated by the lace of falling waters and embroidered with the pearls which constantly drop from the fountain spray'; but today the cumbersome equipment of a defunct sound-and-light show rusts besides the corroded fountain jets, which appear to have dried up for all time; whether they had been turned off because of the 'troubles' and the lack of tourists, or because they were old and a nuisance to maintain, I did not learn.

The use of black marble for the main pleasure house was an astute stroke of genius. From the inside, its dark walls seem remote from the brightness of the exterior world and impervious to heat; from outside, the building, formidable though it is, blends unobtrusively with the heavy chenar shadows. Centuries earlier, of course, the shadow of its dome of pleasure would have floated on the waters of the ornamental pools. As it is, ripples of light reflected from the water bounce around the roof eaves, where, mingled with the flowery decorations of the painted ceiling, is inscribed a famous Persian quotation: 'If there be a Paradise on earth, it is here, it is here, it is here.'

Part of the tradition of renting a houseboat is that one is taken under the wing of the owner and his family, who provide meals and advice and act as 'guides' on any excursion. Mr Guru had been recommended to us by the Jammu and Kashmir Tourist Board in Delhi as being knowledgeable about the Amarnath pilgrimage route in particular. He was a plump and prosperous-looking merchant, with the bustling air of a man who had not enough hours in the day for the conduct of his successful business. He admitted with feeling that with the tourists gone these were terrible times for Kashmir, and yet left us with the impression that he spoke for other, less capable people – he himself, one had no question, had been resourceful enough to turn his hand elsewhere. Something of his consummate entrepreneurial skill was displayed in the adept and lightning-quick manner in which he 'sold' us a guide, a cook, and two pack ponies to conduct us on our trek. He had made the Amarnath pilgrimage twice, although he was Muslim. Somewhat unexpectedly, I witnessed no evidence of antagonism on the part of the Muslim residents of the valley towards the Hindu pilgrims, or vice versa. Every underling in Mr Guru's establishment, it soon transpired, was his son or daughter, and in marked contrast to their father, all were lean and wiry, dark and intense. Of these, Ahmed had been chosen as our cicerone due to his intimate knowledge of the Amarnath route and the history and traditions associated with the pilgrimage; Samson was to be the cook. We were advised that meat was prohibited on the pilgrimage in deference to the

Hindus – again, the matter-of-fact tolerance of, even empathy with, the particular practices of the different faiths was striking.

From Srinagar to Pahalgam, the starting-point of the pilgrimage trek, is a journey of only sixty miles, but one that takes four full hours by car, partly because of the terrain, partly because of the congested army traffic. The road follows the course of two rivers, running first to the southeast with the Jhelum, then, doubling back from the village of Anantnag, running northwest with the Lidder.

The same emotional disjunction aroused in Srinagar by the sight of beauty under siege is accentuated in the countryside, where there is an uneasy juxtaposition between the accoutrements of war and a geography possessed not only of surpassing loveliness, but suggestive of paradisiacal peace. Some of the soldiers, it appeared, had fallen prey to this spell, for while they maintained their assigned posts at one-hundred-yard intervals along the road, they were often to be seen sitting or reclining comfortably under the willow trees that dipped over the roadside canals. The road, which passed through fields of terraced paddy and brilliant saffron, was clogged with slow-moving army vehicles carrying supplies and open-backed trucks piled with soldiers, their rifles pointing nonchalantly ahead of them, i.e. at us. The narrowness of the road prohibited our overtaking them, and so we became unwilling participants in the trundling, exhaust-choked convoy. Dark poplar trees flanked the lanes traversing the fields and formed sentry-straight shadows against the foothills of the distant mountains. While the mountain peaks stood out cleanly and clearly in the pellucid high-altitude air, the towns, villages and road-ways of the valley floor were characteristically tinged with exhaust pollution. This pervasive smog appeared to be a deep-rooted problem caused by more than the relatively recent influx of army vehicles, for streamers of black fumes could be seen trailing behind most private cars and taxi vans.

Every so often, one side of the road was blocked by small boulders, sometimes overseen by sentries, more often not; these appeared to serve more as a reminder of a potential military presence than as an actual deterrent. Sometimes the line of traffic swerved to bypass a donkey cart, or a canopied auto-rickshaw.

On the road itself, Ahmed and Samson were noticeably tense, braced always for a random checkpoint, but in the towns they appeared to drop their guard and to relax. A town's shops stood directly on the thoroughfare, with their dwelling quarters above them. Looking down, sometimes with wistfulness, sometimes with bemusement, from the seclusion of these handsomely shuttered windows were often to be seen the households' women, half veiled, or with veil in hand in readiness to be drawn. Further along the road and higher into the mountains, one came upon villages nestled on some choice spot beneath trees and beside some form of running water, such as a canal, or a stream. The typical burnt-brick and wood architecture of the buildings, with their almost alpine upper balconies and shuttered windows, had the appearance, on this small village scale, of gingerbread houses. The majority of Kashmir's population practises subsistence agriculture, but here in the valley the overwhelming impression was of well-ordered prosperity. The streets, the irrigation channels, the houses themselves appeared strikingly well-tended, and the shop stalls and vendor wagons were piled with fruits, vegetables and pulses. Houses were being built, bricks were being manufactured, fields were being tended. Increasingly, I found myself thinking that the inhabitants of the Happy Valley would manage very well running their own kingdom.

Some twenty miles outside Pahalgam is Achabal, the site of the second of Bernier's gardens, and designed primarily by Nur Jahan, Jahangir's beloved wife. The waters of the Achabal spring have from ancient times been considered holy and spectacular: an account written in the late sixteenth century describes it as 'a fountain that shoots up to the height of a cubit'.

The waters from this still powerful spring are directed into two narrow channels and a broad central one, the latter, as in Shalimar, breaking into a series of ornamental ponds. At the head of the central channel, two small pavilions flank an impressive artificial cascade; the main pavilion forms a little island in the most extensive of the pools. None of these are the original Mogul buildings, but stolid stone structures of a recent date. It has been speculated that on some of the foundations – such as those beside the main cascade – tents or marquees would have been erected rather than permanent buildings. The only Mogul original is set back some distance from the canals, strictly speaking outside the modern boundaries of the garden, and is picturesquely overgrown with wild roses. Inside, bats were whirring round and round in the cavity of its former dome.

The gardens are maintained by the Department of Forestry and Floriculture, and a government fish farm has now taken over part of their territory. The grounds were strikingly well kept, although somewhat marred by modern shrubbery that bespoke the influence of the British raj more than the deft touch of the Moguls. More so than at Shalimar, the gardens of Achabal seem to be a natural extension of the lush and mountainous Kashmiri landscape, in part because of their situation outside a small town as opposed to a dusty city, in part because of the specific nature of the land which presses more closely around them – Achabal spring rises at the spur of the Achabal Thung mountain which directly abuts the far garden wall.

Whereas the tense political situation in Srinagar discouraged casual enjoyment of the Shalimar Gardens, the atmosphere at Achabal was considerably more relaxed. Under the shade of one of the groups of chenar trees, a Hindu family was having a picnic, the two women dressed in tangerine-and-rose-coloured saris, the men in white. Another man joined them, bearing an armful of orange gladioli, which he laid beside the women on the grass. The picnickers were a reminder of another lost feature of the gardens – the handsomely dressed Moguls themselves, strolling the grounds, reclining on their magnificent carpets spread out on the lawns or in their airy tents, or, as Bernier saw, lighting their candle lanterns beside the night waters.

Pahalgam lies at approximately seven thousand feet at the northern end of the Lidder valley, between the junction of the Aru and the Sheshnag, two branches of the majestic Lidder river which flow through defiles at the valley head. Perhaps the most popular of

Kashmir's hill resorts, Pahalgam is well-provided with cheap hotels, restaurants and handicraft stores that once catered to back-packing tourists. Like the houseboat owners, however, most proprietors have closed down their establishments, and although the reappearance of the pilgrims after the two-year hiatus had brought out postcard vendors and caused a few hopeful shops to reopen, the town had the forsaken air of an out-of-season resort. From a selfish point of view, this was entirely desirable, for there can have been few occasions in recent history when the Lidder valley, at the most picturesque and pleasant time of year, was not overrun with trekkers and tourists. Spread along the verdant banks of its rivers, Pahalgam is overlooked by mountains capped with snow and covered with soaring deodar, or Himalayan cedar. The town is not large, and beyond its central cluster of buildings the Lidder rolls through unsullied and spectacular alpine scenery.

The *yatra* is run not unlike a well-organised military campaign, and was in fact overseen by army personnel. Registration took place at the *yatra* headquarters, a tented city of administrative centres, medical and veterinary facilities and tents providing food and shelter. The officer presiding over the registration table told us that it was estimated that six thousand pilgrims would be taking part, a healthy number for any enterprise of this kind, but nothing compared to the tens of thousands of pilgrims who turned up in the years before 'the troubles'.

It was now possible to take stock of exactly what we were letting ourselves in for. The pilgrimage to Amarnath is first mentioned in the *Rájataranginí*, the earliest extant written history of Kashmir, dating from the mid-twelfth century. The pilgrimage follows an ancient peregrine route, and traditionally requires five days. Although the distance to the cave from Pahalgam is only thirty miles, the *yatra* path runs through rough, mountainous terrain that climbs to nearly fifteen thousand feet – the trail is snowbound for the greater part of the year, and is open only from mid-June to mid-October. A brochure published by the Tourist Department of the Jammu and Kashmir Government, under whose auspices the pilgrimage is run, stated that each pilgrim should come equipped with 'sufficient woollens, raincoats, umbrellas, waterproof boots, shoes, walking stick and torch'. Pack ponies and porters were available for hire at an officially established rate, and it was also possible to rent tents, or to make bookings for a space in the tented camps that would be prepared in readiness at the end of each of the traditional stages of the journey. This was all welcome news, making us feel less like over-burdened Westerners with our own pack ponies and tents; in fact, by the day's end, eight thousand *yatris* had turned up, considerably more than had been provisioned for, and both tent space and food was to fall short at the camps.

The pilgrims themselves formed an excited, happy crowd of people from every imaginable walk of life – young executives in shiny dress shoes and mohair sweaters, white-haired women in saris and flip-flops, teenagers in jeans, wild-haired *sadhus* or holy men in nothing at all except for saffron-coloured loincloths. In the *Kedara Kalpa*, one of the sacred texts of Hinduism, Lord Shiva says: 'I am omnipresent, but I am especially in twelve forms and places', one of these being Shri Amarnath. The pilgrimage is not a local affair, or a peculiarly Kashmiri celebration. The *yatris* who had turned up at Pahalgam had come from every part of India: many, unable to afford the air or train fare, had made their way from as far away as Calcutta by travelling for many weeks on local transport. Some pilgrims had made the journey before, but most had not, and, for many, their arrival in Pahalgam this year represented the realisation of a long and fervently held dream.

It is one thing to go trekking in a foreign country, but a different thing entirely to take part in the holy rite of another people's faith, and there was, inescapably, something bogus in our participation. In the *Amareshvara Mahatmya*, an ancient sacred Sanskrit text, however, Shiva instructs his Divine consort, Parvati, saying:

> One who even hears with devotion the story of the pilgrimage, shall be put at par with the one who actually visited the shrine. A visit without full knowledge of the greatness of Lord Shiva would be as futile as incurring the sin of betraying the holy pilgrimage.

As one personally possessed of imperfect knowledge of Lord Shiva, I accepted this warning that my journey would be, in at least one important respect, ultimately futile; but as a teller of the pilgrimage story, I took some encouragement from Shiva's words.

Historically, Hinduism arose in India from the symbiotic evolution of indigenous Dravidian religious beliefs with those imported by the Sanskrit-speaking Aryans who invaded the subcontinent in 1500 BC. There are today well over seven hundred million people of this faith, or over thirteen per cent of the world's religious population. It is one of the most difficult of religions to characterise, for while it possesses a great many sacred texts, it has no paramount 'bible', no hard dogma, no founding figure and no central overseeing authority. This lack of a measure for orthodoxy allows a generous range of beliefs and associated practices. Hinduism holds that all manifestations of the Divine are to be revered, and is therefore markedly tolerant of other faiths; indeed, a Hindu can embrace another religion and still remain a Hindu. Hinduism has been called a religious conglomerate, but this is to overlook the essential unity of its traditions: it is perhaps best regarded as a religious civilisation.

The diversity of Hinduism notwithstanding, it is possible to isolate certain common elements, fundamental among which is the belief in an infinite and eternal transcendent, all-encompassing impersonal principle, called Brahman, the creator generator and preserver of all things, the sole and ultimate reality and both the source and goal of all existences. This is the Absolute, Being-in-itself, which although a principle and not an entity, may be conceived of as a personal god, such as Vishnu, the protector, or Shiva, the destroyer. Other common characteristics are a belief in the authority of the Veda, or ancient Hindu scriptures, and in the Brahmin clans, who are the scholars of the Veda; a respect for all life, of which vegetarianism is a manifestation; and the belief that a person's *karma*, or the sum of his actions in one of his states of existence, determines his fate in other existences, to which the soul transmigrates. This latter belief, as will be seen, is pertinent to the Amarnath pilgrimage.

One of the most important specific forms that Hinduism takes, although more a phenomenon of local folk worship than an orthodox religion, is Shaivism, in which Shiva – as opposed to Vishnu – is regarded as the supreme high god. The Sanskrit word *shiva* means 'auspicious', but the god is revered as both healer and destroyer, the storm god who lashes the land, but who also brings needed rain. Although auspicious, his 'goodwill' cannot be relied upon, and it is this uncontrollable, uncultivated, unreliable aspect of his divine nature that is feared – he is, in this respect, not unlike the Hellenic Apollo. This essential ambivalence is reflected in other aspects of Shiva's nature, for he is both ascetic and lover. For Shaivists, Shiva is the ultimate source and the ruler of all life.

His consort Parvati is also important to the Amarnath story. Parvati was born of mortal parents, the daughter of a Himalayan king, and as a child determined that she would marry no one but Shiva, who was at this time roaming the earth as a mendicant beggar, and living in a cave. When she came of age, her parents attempted to marry her off to wealthy princes, but she resisted. Finally they invited all eligible suitors to their palace for a great party that was to be attended by the gods. Among the guests was Shiva, who appeared first as a prince, then as a beggar. Finally, after Parvati's mother cried out that her daughter would never marry a mendicant, Shiva began his *Thandava* dance; snow began to fall as he shaped the rhythm, then a rain of silver, gold and diamonds. The parents relented, and Parvati and Shiva were married. Their marriage night was celebrated in the cave of Amarnath: this is the abode of Shiva, and it was here that he recounted to Parvarti the secret of creation.

The most important attributes of Shiva are the trident, which represents both his power and his ambivalent nature, and a representation of which is carried at the head of the pilgrimage procession; and the *linga*, or phallus, which with the *yoni*, the female counterpart, is worshipped as representing the creative and generative principles. 'Phallus worship', as this ritual is most conveniently although not strictly accurately called, predates the association of the *linga* with Shiva, and is an example of how a very ancient folk ritual came to be assimilated with a later, dynamic cult. Pilgrimages in general are an important characteristic part of Hindu worship, the sacred sites being typically beside rivers, or in locales of exceptional wild and difficult to reach beauty, such as that for which the Himalayas are renowned.

The Amarnath Cave is a holy and enchanted place not only because of its legendary association with Shiva's marriage – in all likelihood, a secondary 'explanation' – but also because of a striking natural phenomenon. Every year, at the back of the cave, there arises a natural *linga* – a domed pillar of ice rising up to nine feet in height. For the pilgrims, it is the *darshan*, the glimpsing of god. For them, according to the *Amareshvara Mahatmya*, 'every particle of earth, sand and rock, every drop of water and every leaf of vegetation is sacred to this site'. In Shiva's own words, recorded in the same sacred text, 'by seeing and touching Shiva Lingam, uttering mantra, offering flowers, one gets free of all sorts of sins' and incurs 'much wealth, long life, many children, and also fame in this world'. Most importantly, worship at the *linga* releases the pilgrim from the bondage of rebirth; the blessings of the earth can be enjoyed, without the burden of action. This is the 'image of ice' of which Coleridge had read.

> Parama-Shiva is the Shiva-Linga!
> The Universe is the manifestation of this Linga.
> O Sundari! O Devi! O Uma!
> This Lingam is the eternal truth.
> Its darshan will save the liars.
> Its darshan is more meritorious than fasts.
> O Bhairavi! O Parvati!
> It is Sidhi-Lingam!
> It is Buddhi-Lingam!
> It is Sudhi-Lingam!

With the registration completed, we set about finding a site to pitch our tents. Pahalgam is renowned as a shepherds' town – the trails that are so popular with trekkers are in fact made and maintained by the shepherds and goatherds who migrate from mountain pasture to pasture with their flocks. Around Pahalgam itself, the valley's choice thick, springy turf has the appearance of an English country green, but higher upstream it narrows by degrees and becomes rough with boulders; accordingly, the mountainous range that is at some distance from the town centre is dramatically banked on the water's edge higher upriver. We chose a site where the turf was still tame, but the mountains close enough to form a dark, precipitously sloping wall on the opposite banks. Somewhat downstream from us, Ahmed said, was the area that was traditionally marked off as a camping site for the pilgrims.

'*Thousands* of people,' he said. 'Many thousands – you cannot imagine. You would not be sitting here in peace. The tents would be *there* and *there*.' This year, all the pilgrims seemed to be contained within the tented city at the registration compound, or to have gone on ahead to the first official camp of the pilgrimage trek proper. The disparity between what the valley had so recently been and its present appearance was a theme to which Ahmed kept continuously and angrily reverting.

'People will be ruined. They have no money. Only the tourists brought money.' He was insistent that there was no danger for visitors like ourselves, and when asked about the kidnapping of the Israeli tourists, he was contemptuous.

'Tourists? Six Israelis with their heads shaved because they are still in the army, carrying automatic weapons? Tourists? They were part of the team of Israeli advisers the Indian government has been using to help them occupy Kashmir – we have seen many of them around. No tourists have been troubled.'

'The climate of Cashmere is admirably suited to the European,' wrote Major Rennell, an observation that is echoed in the numerous travel memoirs written about the valley, where its temperature, its capacity to grow the fruits and flowers that suit European tastes, its suitability for taking long romantic walks are among its most frequently catalogued assets. Reliance on the tourist dollars of European visitors had, over the years, clearly shaped the economy, the sociology and in small degrees the geography of the Happy Valley – the mossy waters of Lake Negin, for example, have not been cleared because there are no longer people around for whom clear water so badly matters. And yet, ironically, Kashmir itself shaped European assumptions about natural beauty. The glorification of lonely walks in sites of wild and spectacular beauty is central to the Romantic movement, of which, in Britain, Coleridge, with the Wordsworths, was a pioneer. The echo, specifically, of the fountains and disquieting mountains in 'Khubla Khan' is detectable in Shelley's 'Mont Blanc' to give one notable example of Romantic alpine description. The Kashmir landscape is seductive to the European not only because of its astonishing beauty, but because it is part of a familiar poetic landscape that still stirs his soul. When describing our camp-site in my journal that first night, I found myself fighting to resist using the terms that in fact rose most spontaneously to my mind; but how else to capture the savage beauty of the precipitous rockface, dark with cedar pine, slanting athwart the Lidder chasm and its tumultuous waters, than with the dream terms of 'Kubla Khan'?

At dusk, a soldier sauntered over to our camp, and after commenting on the fineness of the evening, pointed into the cedarn shadows of the mountain and warned that there were terrorists lurking there. We built a fire for cooking dinner, but the darkness when it came still seemed immense, as nothing now seemed capable of penetrating the depths of the forest stronghold opposite. The presence of the military forces cast a shadow on our pleasure – the ancestral voices of each side may well be prophesying war.

The first day's march is by far the easiest, being some ten miles along a gently climbing road – in fact, this stage can be made by car or jeep, an option many pilgrims took advantage of. The road to Amarnath follows the Sheshnag or eastern Lidder defile out of the valley. Puffs of yellow dust stirred by the unremitting parade of pilgrims rose in the air and hung above the trail, along which, at this early stage, vendors of incense, postcards, tea, rice and other basic goods had industriously set up business. Shiva's gifts are bestowed upon all *yatris* who worship at his mountain shrine, irrespective of the manner in which they might arrive there, a provision that allows for a striking variety of modes of transportation. Many, like us, went on foot, carrying small packs; far more travelled in cars overloaded with the equipment they would have to reassemble at the end of the road at Chandanwari; many rode patient mules and pack ponies, led by a guide; and a picturesque few rode in dandies, or wooden chairs that are carried aloft Roman-style on the shoulders of four sweating bearers.

Chandanwari lies at an altitude of approximately nine-and-a-half thousand feet, a climb of two-and-a-half thousand feet from Pahalgam, on a road that parallels the Lidder river. With the gentle, shepherds' pasturage of Pahalgam behind, the way becomes dramatically bare and rocky. The pilgrimage road hugged the more benign face of the Lidder gorge, while the opposite face veered off at a precipitously perpendicular angle. Although the gorge reared several thousand feet above us, one thought not of its soaring height, but of its headlong downward plunge to the Lidder river. Streaked with moraines and rock and glacial scars, cluttered with the debris of fallen shattered trees and boulders, every feature on its uncompromising surface evoked not height but giddying depths. In the relentlessly clear sunlight, the cedar pines that stood valiantly rooted against the escarpment's irresistible downward course appeared green-black, and the Lidder itself, far below them, glacial blue. At one point, what appeared to be a marble bridge was seen straddling a torrential passage of water, but was in fact a ridge of compacted perennial snow, and a favourite landmark of the *yatra*.

The option to travel by car or by more traditional means, and the fact that many pilgrims had made their first camp at Chandanwari and not Pahalgam, together ensured that the first day's march was a scattered, disorganised affair, giving little indication of being a unified endeavour. The camp itself had been established in a choice meadow cut by the intersection of two rivers and contoured by mountains: it was here that Shiva once observed a strict thousand-year penance, and the meadow is his Ashram. Another tented city comprised the main, official camp, with army-issue canvas tents set up in orderly lines off a central roadway. Pilgrims with tents of their own, like ourselves, took to the lower meadow by the river, where the most immediately pressing task was to clear the ground, not only of stones, but of the piles of human excrement that dotted this otherwise enticing meadow like cowpats in an extremely well-frequented paddock. A late-nineteenth-century British description of Kashmir had noted that 'picturesque as these pilgrimages are, they have their ghastly side as cholera-conductors', words whose import had not been as compellingly clear to me at the time of reading as they were now. As late as the 1930s, some five hundred pilgrims had died on the Amarnath trek.

At the main camp, the pilgrims had settled into the makeshift routines of a refugee camp. The excess of numbers, unforeseen by the *yatra* authorities, was now woefully apparent, and the sturdy tents bulged with extra camp-beds and were overhung with a haze of smoke. Family groups cooked their food on stoves they had brought with them, or on wood that they had purchased at the camp, while other pilgrims frequented the small restaurant and tea sheds that had been squeezed in among the rank and file of tents. A steady stream of people strolled up and down the main thoroughfare, occasionally stopping to pull back a tent-flap in order to check up on a friend or relative, or looking over the shops. The most ostensible evidence that this gathering of eight-thousand-plus people was for some extra-mundane purpose was furnished by the *sadhus*, who formed a sometimes belligerent, often provocative and always conspicuous presence. These holy men were readily identifiable by virtue of their near-nakedness and their mass of at least waist-length dreadlocks. At the vanguard of the tents, they established their own open-air and very public camp around a single fire, where they sat streaked with ashes and wreathed in wood and ganja smoke. Ganja, or *bhang*, is as universally recognised an attribute of the *sadhus* as their saffron-orange loincloths and meagre cloaks. According to Ahmed, fifty kilos were regularly carried and traded by the *sadhus* on the *yatra*, but this year the 'Kashmir situation' had blockaded their supply lines.

The *sadhu* is a Hindu ascetic, whose indifference to such fleshly concerns as warmth, shelter, and food is exhibited in his lack of clothing, leathered, ash-streaked skin and extreme thinness. If he is a devotee of Shiva, he impersonates Shiva the mendicant, and may carry a small trident or miniature *linga*. The ashes, which when thickly applied give the *sadhu* a harrowed, deathly appearance, are smeared on both for apotropaic purposes and as a symbol of dedication to Shiva. The *sadhus* are central to the Amarnath pilgrimage, and receive a third of the *yatri* offerings; the other two-thirds is divided between the Brahmins and the Maliks, a Muslim family with ancestral rights to the cave. The *Lal Gir Sadhu* leads the procession, and technically speaking is meant to enter the cave first. His white, yurt-like tent, bedecked with saffron banners, is set up at the head of each camp, wherein is guarded the trident of Lord Shiva.

Perhaps owing to the shortness of their ganja supply, perhaps because they well know that they exist safely beyond the pale of ordinary conduct, the *sadhus* seemed in unconcealed ill-temper, and passed the time in baiting the patrolling soldiers. One soldier withstood this treatment for some minutes before barking out a rejoinder, at which, instantly, one of the more aggressive *sadhus* was on his feet, scowling furiously and, having ripped aside the strip of cotton that was his loincloth and only clothing, with dreadlocks streaming to his ankles, attacked the soldier (Beware! Beware! / His flashing eyes, his floating hair!). A sputtering altercation followed, ended only by the loud, laughing and generally insincere remonstrations of the other *sadhus*, following which they all seemed in better spirits.

For this first camp alone, a generator had been rigged up, and at night the overhanging lights enhanced the increasingly carnival atmosphere. We returned to our tent by the river, picking a careful path over the intervening field. Later in the evening, while having dinner in Ahmed's cavernous field tent, we were visited by a young *sadhu*, who sat cross-legged by our camp-fire, gazing at us with disconcerting self-possession. He did not feel the cold, he said impassively, although his most substantial clothing was an elegantly wound tangerine-coloured turban, and no, he did not want dinner. Digging into the cloth satchel he carried on his shoulder, he drew out a small purse, which in turn contained various personal treasures, each of which he displayed with great reverence. Chief of these were a scrapbook of photographs of the holy sites he had visited, inscribed 'Sweet Memories', and his identity pass, good for free rides on public transport, which showed a serious, shaven-headed young man – his mother's son. Mother, father, sister, brother, he had left them all, he said, his infinitely gentle, infinitely vacant eyes rolling upwards, betraying the ganja influence. For five years now, he had not seen anyone he knew. His parents, he reported, were 'delighted'. He fell into silence again, then, some minutes later, quietly slipped away.

The morning brought a stunning sight: thousands of pilgrims squatting in the meadow, relieving themselves before beginning the day's march. Although still early, a busy stream of *yatris* was already on the road. The next camp was only seven-and-a-half miles away, but the journey was reputed to be hard, as from Chandanwari the *yatra* route would be little more than a goat trail, and would climb to twelve thousand feet.

Beyond the camp, the land opened into a rocky valley, whose mountain walls were banded with forest and glacial screes and streaked with rolling water. The trail traced the escarpment edge of the river valley, then cut sharply away and upwards, and for the next hour or so zigzagged mercilessly up the steep rockface. From each new tack of this back-and-forth ascent, one could look up and see tiers of toiling pilgrims on the angular spirals of the trail still above. Now every strength and weakness was displayed to the world: plump city boys puffed and panted, old women climbed at a heroically steady pace, and, in the dainty steps their flip-flop sandals compelled, the *sadhus* drifted by in packs, stopping for impromptu councils and a smoke in the grassy corner of a hairpin bend. Women in saris walked with collapsible umbrellas tied to their backs, carrying plastic bags full of their possessions and, not infrequently, babies on their hips. The overburdened ponies, resigned to suffering, plodded dutifully ever upwards, or were led by overly eager pony men barrelling into and past the other *yatris*. There were mishaps; an overturned dandy spilled out a monstrously fat woman, entangled in the many yards of her sari, and ponies went astray and got stuck on false paths that eventually deadended, and allowed them no room to turn round. The dandy carriers were hired in groups of five, so as to allow one bearer to 'rest' while his fellows took up their burden; but in one astonishing incident, the fifth man flogged his comrades up a particularly steep ascent.

On the lawn-fine grass of the blunt Pisu summit, tea shacks had been set up with the foreknowledge that the hordes of thirsty *yatris* would want a short siesta. Businessmen, students, schoolteachers, widows and widowers, families, the rich, the poor, from every part of India, lay star-scattered on the grass around their spread-out cloths and blankets, a scene which put one in mind, at this height and under the hard clarity of the pristine sky, of a kind of Olympian picnic, rather than a sacred procession. This exposed summit had once been the arena of a titanic fight between the gods and demons. Major Rennell's claim that 'all Cashmere is holy land' is substantiated by the *yatra* map. The land is contoured by the legends attending every stream, river, glacial pool, meadow, pass or distinguishing landmark of any type.

At over eleven thousand feet, we were now above the tree-line, and after the respite of Pisu, the land became harsher, its patches of pasturage fragmented between outcrops of rock and icy streams. As if this change in the landscape were a feature of a more radical shift at some higher and more cosmic level, the weather shifted too and became suddenly harsh. Clouds loomed up, not scudding, but in immovable blocks that banked the sky and settled in. A damp cold descended, and the long line of pilgrims pulled their coats and sweaters and saris tighter about them. Further on, and the land levelled out into an open upland valley, green again, but dull now and unenticing.

Ahead of us, a crowd of pilgrims had gathered on what turned out to be, on drawing closer, the edge of an escarpment that looked down on to the turquoise waters of a glacial lake so opaque as to appear gelatinous. Roughly a mile in diameter at its widest point, Sheshnag lies in an amphitheatre, sunk below the level of the upper valley, surrounded by perilously sheer, snow-capped mountains. Although fed by the many streams that course down its retaining slopes, the glacial waters enter its imperturbable depths with no discernible movement – a stone cast into these waters would not, one imagines, make a splash or ripple, but would be slowly sucked under, as through quicksand. Second only to the Amarnath Cave itself, Sheshnag is the pilgrimage's most important landmark, and is sanctified as the lake on which Shiva sailed with Parvati; in earlier times, pilgrims used to wash away their sins en route to the cave by bathing in its forbidding waters.

Like many rivers and lakes in Kashmir, Sheshnag is also associated with local, more superstitious legends. A *Nág* is one of the old powerful deities, who dwells in the mountains, and who from time to time creeps forth, snake-like, through sinuous passages to emerge in a mountain spring or lake. 'Shes Nag' means 'seven snakes', a reference to the seven peaks that encircle the lake, and to the multiple-headed snake once employed by Shiva to evict a resident, nuisance demon. The snake is still held to reside in the lake, and there was sudden excitement when an obscure object was spotted on its surface by the pilgrims. The crowd began to increase, as more and more people were beckoned over to behold this phenomenon, which George, observing it through binoculars, reported to be a group of ducks.

The sun had long since been neutralised by the clouds. We were at over twelve thousand feet, and the air was raw and cold. The second camp lay only a mile or so distant, and the huddling pilgrims began to trudge on. At one time, the second camp used to be pitched on the flood plain of the amphitheatre, a site now deemed too inconvenient, as well, perhaps, as too close to the lake's haunted waters for night-time comfort. We did not share these scruples, however, and our small entourage descended the slopes to the valley floor.

The most permanent dwellers in this lush, if sodden, enclosure were two families of nomadic shepherds, who had constructed rough summer huts and bouldered sheep pens. They withstood the light but penetrating rain dispassionately, their arms folded under their dark, tattered cloaks, their heads covered only with embroidered skullcaps.

As the rain increased, we pitched our tents and crawled inside, venturing out again only some hours later when it had cleared, George to go fishing in the lake, I to take a walk to the mountains on the far side of our valley basin. The scale of the lake and mountains exceeded the mortal range of perception, and what I had judged to be a short walk across the plain took me over an hour in each direction. The peaks of the barrier mountains were blunted by the heavy clouds and drifted erratically with snow in a manner that suggested no particular meteorological pattern, but an occasional dumping of its burden by an indifferent heaven. The lower slopes were swept with the dark green pasturage that carpeted the valley floor, and silvered with coursing streams that either rolled directly into Sheshnag or, like a *Nág* itself, snaked across the flood-plain from the far mountains before eventually filtering into the unworldly, clouded-blue circle of the lake. Clearly, where I stood now, and the land I had passed through, represented an embodiment of the Romantic ideal of Nature – wild, lonely and formidable. But, perhaps because I was sensitive to my voyeuristic role in this pilgrimage of an alien faith and had become accustomed to view my circumstances with detachment, or perhaps only because I was tired and numb with cold, I felt a strange and disappointing emotional neutrality, a state of mind well known to Coleridge:

> I see them all so excellently fair,
> I see, not feel, how beautiful they are!

I was forced to recognise that, not unlike the pilgrims, I had come expectant of some wild transport of the soul – the poet's *Brahman*. Instead, I found myself roaming the saturated valley floor thinking about a warm fire and my dinner. None the less, in this prosaic state, a kind of purity of perception was forced upon me. Incapable of possessing this scene through some personal emotional transubstantiation – the Romantic poets' 'Intellectual Beauty' – I had to confront and contemplate it as it in fact was, unembellished by flights of poetic or even spiritual fancy – a remote and harsh world that endured magnificently when unseen by human eyes.

Dinner consisted of two trout that George brought back in triumph to the tents, and which we grilled over wood coals. Some of the shepherds paid a visit, but showed little real interest in us. We were transient phenomena, and would pass more quickly than it would take the clouds to clear.

At night, the rain returned and drummed on the tents without abatement into morning. We waited without real hope for a lull in the weather, but eventually gave up and ventured out to break camp and join the other pilgrims. This day's march is the most fearfully anticipated, requiring a long climb up and over the Mahagunas Pass at nearly fifteen thousand feet, before reaching the meadowlands of Panchtarni, the third camp.

Up over the lip of the Sheshnag basin, we came upon Wawjan, the camp in which the pilgrims had passed the rainy night, a grim conglomeration of dripping canvas mired in mud. The *yatra* route had been churned by the feet of the laden pack mules and ponies into a bog too treacherous to negotiate, and instead the pilgrims were fanning out in bedraggled bands across the slopes that overhung the path, following the intricate traces of the myriad goat and sheep tracks that offered surer footing. The valley walls narrowed, and the hill trails became more precipitous, but the main path below, swamped as it was by rivulets running off the mountain, was by now no feasible alternative. The shale slopes blended with the unremitting rain and lowering clouds in an all-encompassing grey fog.

The increasing altitude had, with the devious routes of the goat trails and the weather, considerably slowed the progress of the *yatra*, and we had been walking through steady rain for some hours by the time we began the ascent proper of the Mahagunas Pass. A stiff wind arose, turning the rain into ice, and the clouds moved in yet closer, as if to smother any ray of hope that the day might still be salvaged. Looking about me, I saw no one, with the exception of George and myself, properly equipped for the weather. 'Sufficient woollens, raincoats, umbrellas, waterproof boots/shoes and walking stick . . .' – the pilgrims' efforts to follow the *yatra* organisers' advice were everywhere pathetically apparent: cardigans, sheets of plastic, garbage bags, and fold-up umbrellas were now vainly unfolded against this mere puff of Himalayan might.

An old man wearing a linen safari suit propped himself against the hillslope and spat into the mud, and men and women crouched vacantly, catching their breath in the thin air. Hugging her knees to her chest, a white-haired woman sat in sludge with a sheet of dripping plastic draped over her thin sari. For us too, well-fed and well-equipped though we were, the trek had become a slogging ordeal;

yet, heroically, humblingly, all around us the stream of pilgrims continued in an uncompromising flow, clearly fuelled by an inner fire that we did not possess. Bare feet, flip-flops, plastic slippers, mud-caked socks and canvas tennis shoes slapped and slipped into the mud under carefully held polyester or cotton trousers and trailing saris. I had read in earlier accounts that the Amarnath pilgrimage had through the years exacted its fatalities, but these had seemed to me to be exclusively what they were – reports from another century – and it had never dawned on me that in the modern age a pilgrim might not attain his goal.

Traditionally, each pilgrim on reaching the Pass summit adds a stone to the piles left by those who have preceded him, and so builds a shelter for other pilgrims and the gods. Few people, however, were taking advantage of these crude stone huts: at least the prospect of a fire and warm blankets lay ahead if one continued, whereas there was manifestly no comfort to be had on this wind- and rain-harried platform.

The pebbled moraines of the declining slopes on the other side were now interspersed with grass and, to my amazement, inappropriate as they were to the misery of the day, buttercups and purple Himalayan poppies. The sleet eased to rain as we clambered down the slopes, terraced by goat paths, towards the broad meadowland of the open Panchtarni valley, which was crisscrossed with rivulets and the stone-scattered remains of the beds of rivers now extinct. Five streams, believed to be sacred, drained this flood-plain, and were forded by makeshift bridges of loosely assembled planks. The haphazard descent of the pilgrims, as they spilled into the valley from all directions and all levels of the mountain, resembled some desperate refugee migration, and one was tempted to search into the distance behind them for the sign of an enemy hard upon their heels.

Across the welcome flat land of the meadow, the third camp had been set some distance back from a low embankment overlooking the furthest of the streams. Numbed to the bone with cold, we impatiently pitched our own tents some way in front of this, on the embankment ledge itself. A kerosene stove was lit and its flames allowed to soar outrageously under the capacious roof of Samson and Ahmed's tent, and by slow degrees, we dried off.

As the hours wore on, the rain abated, and towards sunset George called to me from outside the tent to see 'the path to Amarnath'. Impossibly, the weather had cleared, and the sun, slipping into the gorge that lay at the eastern end of the valley, briefly caught the thin stream below us, flaring it with unstable gold. By evening, the heavy clouds had dissipated, and by night only wisps remained in a sky that was crystalline black. The *yatra* is timed so as to bring pilgrims to the cave on the day of the full moon, and by its light the valley mountains could now be seen as the icons of unassailable might one believes the Himalayan peaks to be. In valiant contrast, throughout the rain, its cessation, dusk and evening, the pilgrims continued to flow across the plain, and, as time wore on and the *yatra* thinned out, resumed a single-file formation. Awaking in the night I saw, on drawing back the tent-flaps, snowdrifts gleaming on the towering black peaks and, a long way beneath them, a wobbly line of light from the pilgrims' lanterns descending the far hills and inching across the plain.

The final day's march to the Amarnath Cave, now just under four miles distant, is traditionally begun before dawn. At four o'clock we rose to a softly clouded sky and clear full moon, and an hour later, having packed the tents, made our way out of the valley, following the golden river path of the evening before. At the mouth of the gorge, the trail abruptly left the valley bed in a sharp zigzagging defile into the mountains. The rising light revealed that the day was to be as flawlessly clear as that which had begun our trek. Although accompanying the main body of the *yatra*, we began to pass pilgrims who were already returning, at this early hour, from their worship at the cave. For the first time, this mass migration, this stream of refugees, this confused dispersion, this unwieldy picnic, assumed the unmistakable solemnity of a spiritual event. The narrowness of the mountain defile in the first instance ensured that one truly processed, although the rapt expressions of the returning pilgrims alone bespoke the fact that this communal undertaking had slipped into a new dimension. Their hands clasped before them as if in prayer, their eyes shining and repeating a murmured chant, each returning pilgrim was greeted in Shiva's name with marked reverence by those still en route:

O Bhairavi! O Parvati!
It is Sidhi-Lingam!
It is Buddhi-Lingam!
It is Sudhi-Lingam!

At the top of the defile, the road levelled out into a narrow, gloomy valley, bedded with snow that had drifted up in uneven waves into the close shadows of its walls. In careful single file, the pilgrims crossed the snow-fields, working their way towards the scattered light that filtered in at the far end of this passage. Emerging from the underbelly of the mountain, the blue sky widened again above us, and one saw a river below and up ahead, gaping in the side of the sunlit mountain to the left, the great gulf of the Amarnath Cave.

At the river, the pilgrim men stripped down to their shorts, and the women disappeared discreetly behind stone shelters to undress. The stream of Amaravati descends from a glacier peak to the east, and is the stream by which Shiva bestowed immortality on the other gods. Thin *sadhus*, stout businessmen, sportily dressed youths and elegant women together laid aside their athletic tracksuits, robes, saris, shirts and ties, raincoats and jeans to wash their sins away in the river, and so enter the cave purified. The Amaravati river-bed is rocky and scattered with boulders, and the river valley, although opening up significantly from the snow-fields, is none the less restrictive and steeply banked, with the shadows of its peaks on one side falling across its slopes upon the other. Long drifts of snow and screes of dirt and rubble that had ebbed or avalanched down the mountains revealed the glacial dynamics of the valley. Some pilgrims, either particularly zealous or merely opportunistic, were rigorously brushing their teeth in the sacred waters. Further up the valley, a large 'H' inscribed on the ground with white boulders marked off a helicopter landing pad; it seemed that the Prime Minister had beaten the other *yatris* to it, having arrived for the *darshan* of Shiva Lingam the day before.

A wasteland of massive boulders lay between us and the cave, which yawned above the sacred river, a deep, broad fissure at the 'waist' of the seventeen-thousand-foot-high mountain face. *Amar* means immortal, while *Nath* is a term applied to divinities. It was here

117

that lesser deities pursued by Death had implored Shiva for his protection. He obliged by bestowing on them the waters of immortality, but disappeared shortly afterwards to his own abode. The prayers and petitions of the pilgrims at the cave represent the prayers of the distraught divinities; for mortal pilgrims, Shiva's boon is release from fear of death, not from death itself.

In earlier days, the pilgrims had manifested their lack of consciousness of the physical world by emerging naked from the sacred river and approaching the *lingam* clad only in birch bark. 'One who achieves pleasure in this cave by engaging in the Tandav dance, will be considered pious and equivalent to a god', the *Amareshvara Mahatmya* states, in accordance with which, devout Shaivists used to dance naked about the *lingam*. The mode of worship followed today presents a far more improbable sight – thousands of men and women waiting patiently in a winding queue on rock-cut steps, at nearly thirteen thousand feet, amid snow-capped mountains, for their turn in the carefully controlled access to the cave. Two iron guard railings spanned the cave's 150-foot-wide mouth to channel the entering and exiting crowds, and at its threshold, pilgrims were bade remove their shoes and store them for safekeeping on a convenient shoerack that was overseen by two old men who acted as guards.

The damp stone was as cold as ice beneath our feet, as we inched towards the deeper recesses of the cave. Although packed together, and by necessity virtually stationary, the extraordinary agitation of the pilgrims' faces conveyed an impression of restless movement in the crowd: anticipation, trembling zeal, sheer bliss – the ferment of many souls was written nakedly on the expectant faces. A contained roar of voices and the clapping of hands made me turn, and following the crowd's pointing fingers and uplifted hands I saw pigeons sailing out from a niche in the cave roof some one hundred and sixty feet above us, into the sunlight of the valley. These are the manifestations of Shiva and Parvati, which the ancient texts claim with confidence will play a part in each *darshan*.

We had ascended the steps as far as a stone platform with a marbled surface and the entrance to the sanctum sanctorum of the inner cave, which was flanked on each side by *sadhus* – the one on the left, engrossed in a holy book, the one on the right, receiving cash offerings. At this point, a large bell was vigorously rung by each pilgrim as he mounted the platform. Set some distance away from the steps was a small shrine consisting of statues of Shiva, Parvati and a black stone *lingam*, before which many, but not all, of the pilgrims prostrated themselves, touching each object with reverential hands. Higher up the marbled steps, in a niche between the cave and the platform, lay two more *sadhus*, sprawled in a web of orange scarves and paper money.

A high iron grille rose from the back of the platform, almost obscuring from view the ice *lingam*, which could just be glimpsed behind it. The old man immediately in front of me finally succeeded, after many attempts, in lighting a stick of incense with trembling hands. We drew even with the rail, and at last confronted the miracle of ice – a milky-yellow column some seven feet in height, festooned with scarves and tinsel and scattered with rose petals. Delicately preserved beneath its surface lay the offerings of past years – leaves and yellow, white and red flower petals that had been trapped in the clouded ice with the thawing and re-formation of the *lingam*. Two soldiers waved us on: eight thousand people are a lot to monitor, and the moment of religious ecstasy must be carefully rationed. Passing before the shrine, each pilgrim received the *tilaka*, the red forehead mark worn by the devout Hindu, from the hands of one of the soldiers.

Guided by the guardrails, we processed along the back of the cave, passing a long, low ledge of ice. The official story of the ice is that Shiva melted himself and then froze into a *lingam* for the amusement of Parvati, who worshipped him in this form. A more prosaic, and less suggestive, explanation is that several springs issue forth from the back of the cave, and due to the peculiar formation and pressure of their fissures, well up in a manner that forms the distinctive ice masses.

From the rock wall above the ledge of ice, a small group of successful pilgrims was busily chipping away souvenirs. Shoes were reclaimed and the custodians tipped. Outside, and looking back from the head of the sacred river, Amarnath loomed as a massive, unadorned black hole between heaven and earth. These glacial monuments! This fissure in the Mesozoic dolomite! This cave of ice! Better, surely, to rush disorderly and naked from the river than worship in the rank and file of rock-cut steps and careful guardrails!

In the sunshine of the valley, many of the pilgrims now allowed themselves a well-earned break. Washing was done in the stream, food was unpacked, photographs were snapped, and naps taken on patches of turf amid the boulders. Many, however, immediately commenced the long road home. This day's march was in fact the hardest, continuing back through Panchtarni to the camp at Sheshnag, in all a distance of nearly sixteen miles, and over the Mahagunas Pass. We arrived at our former glacial camp in the late afternoon almost on our knees with exhaustion. But the night sky was as clear as the day's, and we were rewarded by the sight of milky Sheshnag lake under the full clear moon.

We encountered only a scattered remnant of the *yatra* on the next day's journey to Pahalgam. With their goal attained, the pilgrims could indulge in a leisurely pace, and the relatively few people we passed were strolling along easily, or, especially if they were older, dozing in the sun on the grassy wayside. If indeed the *darshan* of Shiva Lingam brings an end to the soul's cycle of transmigration, then this was for them the end of the journey that would end all journeys.

In a letter to his old friend Robert Southey, Coleridge, in a wave of nostalgia, suggested that 'a Poet might make a divine allegory' of their parallel journeys through life. 'O Southey ... a spiritual map with our tracks as if two ships had left Port in company.'

The Amarnath *yatra* is the stuff of spiritual epic, and a poet could well make an allegory, divine or otherwise, of the parallel journeys made by the pilgrims and myself as we followed our different spiritual maps, like the song-lines of unrelated tribes. And as the value of a map is determined by how well it gets a person to his destination, I would have to allow the superiority of the pilgrims' – little else could account for the heroic completion of this arduous trek by so many elderly and frail, ill-equipped men and women who, often by their own admission, in normal circumstances never walked as much as a straight mile.

Yet, in the grand picture, I am not convinced that the map of either of our tracks, or both together, adequately and completely describes the terrain we trod. The truest manifestation of the miracle of ice, bare of tinsel, guards and patient crowds, may well be that which none of us will ever see. For which reason, when I build that cave of ice in my imagination, I envisage a winter journey, when the valleys would be white, Sheshnag lake a frozen opaque sheet and Amarnath Cave drifted with snow and hung with ice beneath the sunny dome of the blue Kashmiri heavens; I see it as it must in fact appear during those iron months of winter when its paths are blocked, and access is forbidden even to the hardy shepherds.

MOUNT
ABORA
(AND THE
ABYSSINIAN
MAID)

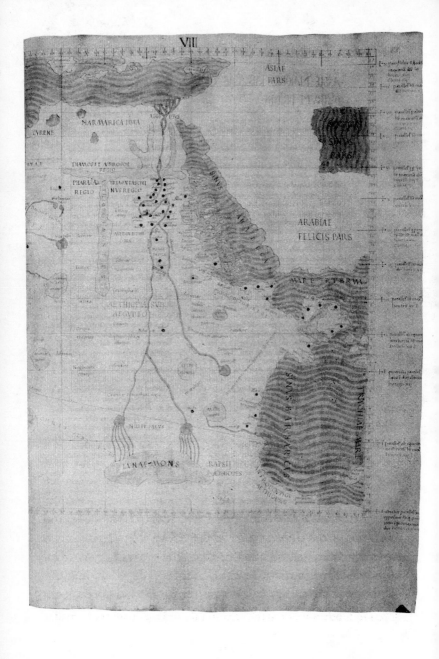

Mount Abora
(and the Abyssinian Maid)

One of the books most widely read at the close of the eighteenth century, John Livingston Lowes tells us, was the Scottish traveller James Bruce's *Travels to Discover the Sources of the Nile*, a work that has been called the 'epic of African travel'. Published in 1790, it is the highly romantic account of Bruce's six-year journey to and from the source of the Blue Nile in Ethiopia. From the evidence of another of Coleridge's poems ('Religious Musings'), a Notebook memo and his correspondence, we know this was a work that made a great impression on him. The memo, for example, outlines his idea of using the seeking of the 'fountains of the Nile' as a poetic motif. Bruce's description of the Ethiopian landscape and of his first sighting of the two fountains emerging from a 'little island of green sods', a place held sacred by the local people, has, as will be seen, strong resonances with both Bartram's Florida and Kashmir, and almost certainly motivated the conception of the 'sacred river' of 'Kubla Khan'.

Abyssinia is referred to more directly, of course, in the weird and wonderful concluding cadenza of the poem:

> It was an Abyssinian maid,
> And on her dulcimer she played,
> Singing of Mount Abora.

It should be noted here that the earliest known version of 'Kubla Khan', that of the Crewe Manuscript now in the British Museum, differs in subtle ways from the version that was eventually published.

One of these textual divergences is of crucial importance to the issue at hand: in the manuscript, it is not 'Mount Abora' but 'Mount Amara' of which the Abyssinian maid sings, the later revision in all likelihood being made in the interest of euphony (A*b*yssinian/A*b*ora).

We know, then, that Coleridge was, through Bruce, predisposed to things Abyssinian, and it is therefore likely that another memorable account of Abyssinia contained in Purchas' *Pilgrimage* – the work Coleridge had on his lap when he fell into the reverie that brought the world 'Kubla Khan' – would have caught his attention; and in light of the manuscript evidence, it seems reasonable to suppose that a chapter entitled 'Of the Hill Amara', based on a report by the Spanish Friar Luys de Ureta, particularly captured his imagination. This is all the more probable given Purchas' extravagant introduction:

> Many, many other Æthiopian rarities we might observe out of this Author; but (if it deserve credit) the Hill Amara after his description, may furnish you far and beyond all the rest of Ethiopia, as a second earthly Paradise.

Friar Luys, we soon learn from Purchas, never actually saw Amara, and his account is taken from that of a fifteenth-century writer, who reportedly spent some time on the Hill in the service of the emperor of his day. By way of introduction to his report, we are reminded by the author that, according to Homer, the gods banqueted in Ethiopia and at this time bestowed on Amara the fruits of their collective gifts. Thus, the Hill, 'situate as the navil of that Ethiopian body' on a great plain, is endowed with the choicest of gardens, temples and art. The hill is round and circular, and requires 'a daies worke to ascend from the foot to the top'. The rock sides are cut so smooth and straight that it 'seemeth to him that stands beneath, like a high wall, whereon the Heaven is as it were propped'. A pleasant stream waters the gardens, leading eventually to a lake. On the summit are thirty-four sumptuous palaces 'where the Princes of the Royall bloud have their abode', having been consigned to the hill fortress from the age of eight for the rest of their lives, so as to be safely out of the way of the ruling monarch, and thus ensure 'that one Sun only may shine in that Ethiopian throne'.

Among the many features of Amara that would have been sure to have appealed to Coleridge were the twin temples to the Sun and Moon, material for his endlessly projected *Hymns to the Sun, the Moon, and the Elements*; the 'sweet flourishing, and fruitfull gardens' which, burgeoning as they are with Oranges, Citrons, Limons, Cedars, and Palme-trees, are reminiscent of Bartram's gardens of Nature; and, unmatched in the world, the wonderful library attached to the Monastery of the Holy Cross, a collection based on the Queen of Sheba's private library, with lost works by such valuable authors as Solomon, Abraham, Job and the Greek Fathers.

The unconfirmed, second-hand nature of Friar Luys's account becomes increasingly apparent as this wonderful narrative progresses, but there are, none the less, threads of truth woven into its glittering fabric. In 1270, the powerful northern Zagwe dynasty was over-thrown by Yekunno-Amlak, who established in its place an Amharic 'Solomonic' dynasty of his own. His death only fifteen years later precipitated a squabble for power among his many sons; and some time during the years 1293 and 1299, 'Mount Amara' was indeed established as a prison for princes of the ruling line.

In the early sixteenth century, invading Muslim forces under the command of Ahmad Gran swept down from the Shoah plateau into the mountainous passes that led into Amhara, where the royal forces had made a last retreat. In the years subsequent to the Solomonic dynasty's rise to power, Amhara had served as the unof-ficial capital of an increasingly strong Christian empire, and as such now bore the brunt of Ahmad's anti-Christian hostility. All the great churches and thriving monasteries were sacked and their manuscripts, art and treasures burned and looted. Muslim chronic-les of the time report an attempted siege by Ahmad's forces of the rock citadel of Amara, on which could be seen 'a thousand palaces'. The mountain citadel, after holding out for months, succumbed at last, and its buildings were burned to the ground. It was the last time that Mount Amara served as a royal prison.

Its use as a monastery, however, continued, and over the centuries successive replacements of the mountaintop churches of which Coleridge had read in Purchas were safeguarded by battalions of priests of the Ethiopian Orthodox Church, a distinctive and ancient branch of Christianity, most closely related to that of the Copts. Whether there remained any relics of the royal past, or of the days when the gods banqueted on its heights amid gardens and fountains, or of the matchless treasures of its library, remained to be seen. But, from what I could gather, an isolated monastery was still in existence on the summit of Gishen Mariam, as the Hill of Amara is now called, in the remote and desolate tablelands of north-central Ethiopia. This and the fountains of the Blue Nile were my next two destinations.

As Purchas indicates, the land of the Ethiopians was known as far back as Homer's *Iliad* – one theory for the origin of its name is a derivation from the Greek *aithein ôps*, meaning 'to burn the face'. With a total area of over four hundred and seventy thousand square miles, Ethiopia is the ninth largest country in Africa. Its boundaries are shared in the south with Kenya, in the west with Sudan, and in the east with both Djibouti and, traditionally a troubled border, Somalia. Formerly its northern boundary had been its six hundred miles of coastline along the Red Sea, but a lengthy secessionist war which, in May 1991, achieved independence for Eritrea, formerly its northernmost province, has imposed upon Ethiopa a new international northern border.

Uniquely in sub-Saharan Africa, Ethiopia was never colonised: an invading Italian army that attempted to stake a claim on the country in 1896 was resoundingly beaten by indigenous forces led by Menelik II – an event which gained Ethiopia marked prestige throughout the rest of the continent – and had to content themselves with the small northern province of Eritrea, which they established as a colony. Modern Ethiopia did not come into existence until the mid-nineteenth century; prior to this, its rule had been divided among different petty kingdoms. Its earliest recorded civilisation dated from the second millennium BC: the kingdom known as Punt to the ancient Egyptians. The aboriginal inhabitants of the land are believed to have been of Hamitic stock, related to the Berbers of North Africa and the ancient Egyptians. In the sixth century BC, a south Arabian Semitic people immigrated to Ethiopia and for the next seven centuries, this 'Sabaean' culture was the dominant influence. Amharic, the national language of modern Ethiopia, is a Semitic tongue.

In the second century AD, the powerful kingdom of Aksum arose in the north, originating, according to tradition, from Menelik I, the offspring of Solomon and the Queen of Sheba, and characterised in many important respects by Judaism of that time. Christianity was brought to Ethiopia in the fourth century AD, and in spite of Islamic incursions which began in the seventh century, has remained in strength to the present day, giving it one of the longest unbroken histories in Christendom. As a Christian stronghold in a continent that, in European eyes, was otherwise inhabited by pagans and Muslim infidels, Ethiopia came to be romantically regarded as the lost kingdom of the legendary Christian ruler, Prester John. Isolated from their mainstream counterparts by an enveloping hostile Arab presence, local politics, and the challenging nature of the country's mountainous terrain, Jewish and Christian sects evolved their own unique, Ethiopian character. The religious practices of the Falasha, or Ethiopian Jews, appear to derive directly from the patriarchal traditions of the Old Testament; the Ethiopian Orthodox Church believes in the Monophysite, or single, divine nature of Christ, as opposed to the more widely held doctrine of human/divine duality.

The Portuguese were the earliest Europeans to gain a foothold in the country, largely in the form of missionaries who were bent on converting the country to a more orthodox, i.e. exclusively Catholic, form of Christianity. The Jesuits were expelled in 1633, but a Portuguese presence remained influential throughout the Gondar period, so named from the powerful city-state which dominated Ethiopia from this date until 1855. Modern unification of the kingdom's disparate and contentious factions began at the close of the Gondar period and continued until the death of Menelik II in 1913. The country's internationally best-known ruler, the Emperor Haile

Selassie ('the Lion of Judah', 'the King of Kings') came to power as regent in 1917, and as Emperor in 1930. Under Selassie's courageous leadership, Ethiopia endured a brief, and wholly illegal occupation, by Mussolini's forces from 1935 until its liberation by the Allies in 1941. The effect of the earlier Italian presence in Eritrea, however, was to be more lasting. At the end of the Second World War, this former Italian colony was placed under British administration until 1952, when it was federated with Ethiopia; ten years later, it was formally annexed as a province. Rebel forces fighting for a liberated Eritrea arose immediately afterwards, and continued to plague successive Ethiopian governments up until their *de facto* victory in May of 1991.

After the Second World War, Selassie continued his earlier attempts to modernise his kingdom. His attention, however, was largely focused on the urban centres, while the countryside remained in the thrall of a virtually medieval feudal system. In 1973, a famine in the northern provinces that resulted in the loss of at least one hundred thousand lives served to fuel an increasing discontent with the country's leadership. In the wake of a wave of popular strikes and mutinies within the army, Selassie was deposed in 1974. A governing national committee called the Derg (literally 'committee' in Amharic) was established, its membership drawn from the military ranks. Members of the old imperial guard were spirited away, to imprisonment and often death. The emperor's murder followed in 1975, according to most sources by the command, if not the actual hand, of his eventual successor, the sinister Colonel Mengistu Haile Mariam.

With the aid of Soviet backing, Mengistu's Marxist government took a stranglehold grip on the country, which it increasingly terrorised by acts of organised, wanton cruelty. Rebel armies, together with those fighting for the independence of Eritrea and the neighbouring state of Tigré, engaged the Derg forces in unabating civil wars, and on 21 May 1991, Mengistu at last bowed to necessity, and fled the country. Freed from the tyranny of his presence, investigators have begun dredging up past atrocities committed by his regime, and mass graves of his victims have been exhumed. The

Ethiopian People's Republic Democratic Front (EPRDF), the current ruling party, have – ambitiously – called for complete democratisation of the country by the end of 1994, which, if successful, will be among the first in the African continent. When I arrived in Addis Ababa, the Ethiopian capital, less than a year after the dramatic events of May 1991, I found people everywhere talking politics, everywhere both optimistic and anxious, holding their breath to see how the next chapter of the country's history would be written.

Addis Ababa stands at an altitude of 7600 feet above sea level in the western highlands, one of the three major geophysical regions into which the country can be divided, the other two being the eastern highlands, which is abutted by important upland plains, and the rift valley and lowland region, riddled with lakes and still active volcanoes. At elevations ranging from nearly eight to twelve thousand feet, the highland climate is temperate, and at night and during the aftermath of heavy rain, downright cold.

Stripped down to the bare bones of its architecture and physical layout, the core of Addis would be seen to possess a kind of heavy Victorian elegance, conceived on an old-fashioned grand scale, with its tree-shaded boulevards and wide commercial streets, the National Palace set behind grandiose iron gates in sweeping grounds, the old railway station and the monumental Lion of Judah. As it is, however, the city has to accommodate a population of nearly three million, which has been accomplished only by squeezing in, wherever space permits, an array of distinct settlements bearing no resemblance to the pre-existing communities beside which they nestle. Whole sections of the city have grown up like separate villages along the pot-holed or unpaved roads leading off to the better residences. At the far end of the lavish grounds of the Addis Hilton there sprawls a confused, brown shantytown, spread shakily under corroded iron roofs on muddy ground.

Knots of armed soldiers, usually positioned at strategic corners, were a common sight, although at this time not an overtly hostile presence. The end of the civil war had brought with it an aftermath of unsettlement, with two opposing armies essentially at a loose end and no one clearly in control of both. A curfew was still very much in effect at the time of my arrival: my hosts on the first evening had, just the night before, incurred three bullet holes in their car as a result of returning home late from a dinner party. (However, they complained to the security forces and received a formal apology and assurance that the cost of repairing the car would be met by the authorities.) In general, people seemed remarkably talkative and open for a population that had been, for seventeen long years, essentially under gag rule and patrolled by spies. A demonstration several thousand strong processed peacefully up Menelik Avenue on my first day in Addis, a parade made picturesque by the colourful parasols many marchers carried. No one I asked knew the specific cause of the demonstrators, but as one bystander told me, 'Everyone now has something to say.'

My immediate concern was to inquire about transportation. Broadly speaking, Lake Tana in the western highlands is referred to as the source of the Blue Nile; Bruce's quest, however, had led him to the specific point at which the lake's tributary first makes its appearance aboveground, at a place called Gishe Abay some distance south of Tana itself. There were a number of ways of getting to Bahar Dar, my first destination and the town closest to Lake Tana – by air or a two-day bus journey, for example – but the extra leg to Gishe Abay was more problematic. Petrol supplies in Bahar Dar were unreliable and there could be no guarantee that I would find local means of reaching the Nile fountains. As for Gishen Mariam, four-wheel-drive transportation of some kind was an absolute necessity, the mountain road being by all reports rough at the best of times, and currently in a very poor state of repair. Again, local transport could get me as far as Dessie, the capital of Wollo district in which Gishen Mariam lay; transport – and petrol – from Dessie to the monastery, however, proved impossible to requisition in advance. All local four-wheel-drive vehicles were in the possession of the number of relief agencies that operate out of Dessie, and their priorities, reasonably, did not include day trips to mountaintop monasteries of poetic interest. Nor was it possible to rent a vehicle in Dessie itself, which meant that my best bet was to finalise all transactions beforehand in Addis.

The transportation dilemma is worth spelling out in detail because it is illustrative of the kind of very basic infrastructure problems that Ethiopia faces, and helps to explain its earlier attitude to tourism. In the past, a visitor had to submit every aspect of the most modest itinerary to the scrutiny of a single government agency, the notorious National Tourist Organisation, or NTO. Even a short excursion within the Addis city limits would require the presentation of a list of specific destinations and advance payment at an extortionate rate for a car and driver for a specified block of time. Individual tourism anywhere outside Addis was also made as difficult and as expensive as possible, and required a battery of official permits for pre-approved routes. Today, one can travel freely from district to district with a minimum of bureaucratic hassle. Rented transportation is still astronomically expensive, but, one has to acknowledge, understandably so: in spite of the rough terrain and roads, there are few four-wheel-drive vehicles in the country in the first place, and the petrol supply is a chronic problem, especially in view of the daunting number of uses to which it must be put in the interest of rebuilding the battered nation. As a result of this new attitude towards tourism, envisaged as a not unimportant component of the rebuilding effort, a number of private tour companies have opened up, breaking the NTO monopoly. After extensive inquiries, a small company called Caravan Tour and Travel looked the most promising; unusually, it was run by a woman.

Samia Saleh Kebire was a beautiful, extremely elegant woman in her mid-thirties, with a face that radiated intelligence and a manner that indicated a can-do, entrepreneurial talent. In addition to running her business, she had three children to raise, the offspring of a marriage her parents had arranged for her at the age of seventeen to a considerably older man, who, for his part, had determined to make her his wife when he had first met her four years beforehand. This matrimonial method had, in Samia's case, something to recommend it, for seventeen years down the line, the marriage was clearly a very happy one. A photograph I later saw of Samia showed her in traditional Tigrayan dress – robed, veiled, her eyes heavily kohled and with a sweeping gold ring through her nose. She was excited and intrigued by my trip, never having heard of, let alone been to, my specific destinations. Her enthusiasm visibly increased with each meeting, and I knew that she was doing extensive homework behind the scenes. Having put myself in her hands, I was told to relax and look around the city while she negotiated petrol supplies, drivers and boat time on the lake through her considerable network of contacts.

'I am thinking it is better that I go with you to Bahar Dar,' she said after a couple of days, with studied nonchalance. 'That way I can see that everything is in order. Because this is special, I do not want to leave it to the boys.' The boys, it would turn out, were her string of grown male employees.

Relieved of all responsibilities, I passed a few desultory days in Addis, taking in all the 'sights' – the National Museum housed in Haile Selassie's former palace, the market, the shops, the grandiose Soviet-style Revolutionary Square – pacing the streets often in drizzle, as this was the beginning of the season of rain. The swimming pool at the Hilton was built over a hot spring, and I availed myself of this amenity on a daily basis. It was in the nearby coffee shop that I came across a television schedule and learned that CNN was available around the clock and that Agatha Christie's *Death on the Nile* was being shown that night.

I was staying in a rambling, pleasantly seedy, colonial-looking hotel set in gardens and conveniently central to the town. The somewhat gloomy lobby was invariably filled with crowds of foreigners, mostly on business. The majority were lone Europeans, whose eyes tended to search out each new white face looking for possible contact, or, alternatively, to avoid it studiously. A caftaned West African strode in escorted by a flotilla of enormous, turbaned women, who were jointly received by the Ethiopian hotel staff with noticeable distaste. A professionally charming Rasta man held permanent court, usually either waiting for or entertaining journalists: Ethiopia is, of course, the Rastafarian Zion, and there is a small settlement of Jamaicans south of Addis. And more and more visitors . . . who were all these foreigners crowding Prester John's lost kingdom?

In the hotel lobby I also learned of the curious fate of a local hermit, one of the many holy ascetics who live the lives of biblical prophets in various parts of the Ethiopian wilderness. The man in question was on the eve of departure for America, having had the dubious good fortune to have been the object of the visionary dream of a Californian woman. Her dream had been of *this particular prophet* – or so the woman claimed, and she had been told that he would be the salvation of herself along with a great many other people. Abandoning her ties with the Pentecostal Church, she had converted to the faith of the Orthodox Abyssinians, and had come to Ethiopia on a dream and a prayer to take the hermit home with her to California; to do what, no one knew, as she spoke no Ethiopian language, and the prophet no English.

In Addis, the Ethiopians I met were well-informed about the West; all who could had followed the Gulf War on CNN with passionate attention, and they were remarkably up-to-date on the upcoming American presidential election. I, on the other hand, became increasingly aware of my cursory knowledge of Ethiopian history – there had been Haile Selassie, and of course the Italians, and some very bad years, and now things were much better. And so again, in Prester John's legendary realm, I found the tables turned.

'The new countries do not interest me so much,' Samia would later tell me, wrinkling her nose. I had asked if she had any desire to visit America. 'Me, I prefer the ancient cultures, like in Italy. I adore Italy. Have you been to Cortona? No? But it is so near Florence. It is one of my favourite places in the world.'

On the morning of our departure, I was woken by a woman's voice, strident, indignant and English, rising from the garden below my window. 'What do you mean, you don't know what it is? It's your national *bird*.'

In the breakfast room, every window table was taken by a solitary European with a book propped up in front of him. At the centre tables, Africans sat in couples animatedly talking business, or in family groups.

After breakfast, while buying postcards at the small hotel giftshop, I ran across the owner of the voice that had awoken me, a thin, drawn-looking Englishwoman who was taking her leave, reluctantly it seemed, of the Ethiopian woman who ran the shop.

'Yes. Well, I enjoyed the coffee,' she said in a somewhat haughty, piercing English voice.

'You can come back. Don't worry, we can do it again,' the proprietress replied languidly, cutting through the shrill diffidence to the lonely, displaced core.

The arrangements made by Caravan Tour and Travel on my behalf included flying to Bahar Dar from Addis. At the airport, the sky was lowering and stormy. When our flight was announced, Samia and I filed out with the other passengers on to the tarmac where two planes were awaiting, their gangways down. One was absurdly small and propellered, the other a tidy, miniature jet. I marched decisively towards the latter.

'It is this one over here,' Samia called to me from under the wings of the first plane, where the eight other passengers were regarding me curiously from the gangway ladder. We were delayed from take-off while attempts were made by the land crew to hunt down a spare Ethiopian Air official to enact the duties of flight attendant on the spur of the moment. Wise men all, they had placed themselves well out of sight, and an hour passed before a candidate was driven up the gangway, and the plane's tiny door closed inexorably behind him.

The weather was judged to be holding and we were cleared for take-off, although there was the chance that an in-flight route change might deposit us some place other than the scheduled destination. Bad weather made this standard rainy-season procedure.

'Ethiopian Air is the best airline in Africa,' I recited to myself as we took off, an incantation that was in fact true. Outside Addis, the mountainous slopes that fell away from the city were thickly wooded and I realised with a start that this forest coverage had once been extensive – that this was what, in a more generous age, the land had looked like where it was now plucked bare. The plane danced and slipped in the sky and I cast a covert glance at Samia who was leaning back in her chair composedly, albeit with her eyes closed. I was quietly sick in my airline bag, something I had never succumbed to before.

'It is because we are sitting near to the front of the plane, over the propellers,' I explained to Samia, who raised her eyebrows and slowly nodded. Below us, under thunderous, careering shadows, the earth was parched and brown, rent here and there by massive abysmal clefts and canyons whose depths showed only as dark patches from the clouds. An eternity later, I opened my eyes to find that the day had become brisk and sunny, and that we were skittering towards a great lake.

I leaned towards my window, hoping to catch a glimpse of the Nile, here at the commencement of its 2750-mile course to the Mediterranean. A dirty brown but none the less impressive river could be seen winding across the plain that spread outside the town we were now approaching. Skirting its shore, our flight revealed that the water of Lake Tana was – truly – eau-de-nil, pea soup turning abruptly to deep coral-reef blue around its jagged jetties of land.

'What is wrong with this picture?' I wondered to myself, as we touched down and coasted towards the terminal building. Its right side was slouching and it was in general bad repair, but there was something else amiss that I could not immediately put my finger on. Drawing closer, the 'building' was revealed to be a lone façade; behind its one surviving wall lay only charred rubble.

'The fighting was very bad here, all around Bahar Dar,' said Samia. 'The people really suffered.' The airport had been bombed and all that remained usable was the runway on which we had landed. The plane's luggage was unloaded while we talked and piled on to a cumbersome trolley, which was then manually and laboriously dragged up the road leading from the airport. The labourers in question were not in uniform, but I assumed these were official duties they had undertaken; even the formality of a luggage trolley seemed under the circumstances a miracle of courtesy.

A group of cars and vans waited some distance up the road to claim the passengers – another token of unorthodox efficiency. Samia's requisitioned van was among them, and two of her 'boys' were on the lookout for her. I sensed affectionate deference to her in their greeting.

The land was now very flat, and the heat fierce, or perhaps it only seemed so after Addis. There was little traffic, and the roads were used less by cars than by pedestrians, most of whom were dressed in shabby Western clothes and barefoot. Some of the men had draped their heads with long bands of cloth resembling clumsy turbans, presumably as protection against the heat.

Bahar Dar lies on the southern shores of Lake Tana, and has historically been one of the Ethiopian towns on a visitor's itinerary – always assuming that the current political situation made such visits feasible. Its major attraction is the lake, but the town itself is not unattractive. Its outskirts are fringed with high grass, palms, eucalyptus and banana trees. The simple mud-brick houses and shops are brightly painted, the roads wide and clean and the central road, at least, well paved. On entering the town, one is confronted with an enormous billboard with crude but effective paintings of a distraught woman, a broken human body and the head of Mengistu. One did not have to be able to read the lurid Amharic subscript to know that this was a testament of outrage against the thousands upon thousands who were tortured and killed by the Derg forces. The toll in Bahar Dar was by all reports especially bad. Everyone seemed personally to know of someone who had suffered.

The first day's programme included a tour of the town, and then a drive up into the nearby hills along a snaking road shaded by jacaranda and flamboyant trees and scattered with their lavender and red petals. We came to a halt in a sweeping circular drive adjacent to a promontory that looked out over the Blue Nile valley and Lake Tana some distance away to the east. The drive behind us, as it turned out, marked the entrance to a grand house, guarded by an armed sentry and iron gates, that in happier days had been Haile Selassie's residence.

Below us, a band of lush grass on either side of the river marked its flood-plain. On the far shore, a faint haze of woodsmoke hung over the trees and villages, blending easily into the benign, grey twilit sky. In the light wind, the river surface was roughened into silver scales, but showed no movement at all of its own – without reference to the lake one could not have guessed in which direction it was flowing; but in a different time of year, between November and March, this same river would be raging over the valley. While the White Nile, which has its origin in Lake Victoria in Kenya, is the longer river, the Blue Nile accounts for over seventy per cent of their combined water volume, a fact that gives one an idea of the extent of its full, rainy-season strength. In 1990, this peaceful scene had been marred by a battle. The bridge leading to Bahar Dar had been blown up by guerrilla forces and some of Mengistu's troops who were left stranded on the far shore had attempted to ford the river at its height. Mired by mud, overwhelmed by its deceptively powerful current and for the most part incapable of swimming, as many as three hundred men are thought to have drowned, and their bodies still lie somewhere on the bed of the Blue Nile. Indeed, the promontory, backed as it is by the Lion of Judah's 'palace', puts one in mind of the kind of platform from which a latter-day Xerxes might survey his troops. One could well imagine the little Emperor's sombre pride and satisfaction in surveying this scene – one of the world's mighty rivers at his feet, and the sound of his subjects' voices rising as shrill as a bird's cry from the plain.

There was time enough before dark to drive to the lake, where we found fishermen congregated under the boughs of an enormous, friendly tree, chatting together in the dusk. Their boats, made of bundles of papyrus reed, had been dragged on to the shore and overturned to dry out overnight – each boat has a lifespan of about three good fishing days. Two little boys who had followed us to the boats stepped forward to report with some eagerness that historians now believe that the ancient Egyptians learned the art of making their papyrus crafts from the Ethiopians, and not, as was formerly held, vice versa; this same information was to be conveyed to me on a number of occasions, and so it is clearly a matter of national pride. Papyrus reeds had also been used to build the rough shacks in which some of the lakeshore people lived. Lines of mules were being laden with corded bundles of cut wood that had been ferried over by these lightweight boats from the other shore. By the time we left, the night air was heavy with the scent of wood fires, a textured scent, resinous and grainy like good honey, that I have always associated with nightfall in Africa.

I had been booked into the Ghion Hotel, one of the two lakeshore establishments. The small complex of low buildings had been built by the Italians and used as their regional headquarters during the period of their occupation. It had been 'destroyed', I was told by a local resident, in 1989 or so by the fighting, and so the mustardy-yellow and green walls, the tiny central garden, the swept paths and flower-beds were all evidence of its valiant resurgence.

In the forlorn dark television room, the television was tuned in to the national station which repeatedly broadcast events relating to the recent, unthinkable events. It was rumoured that in the final, increasingly paranoid months of the Derg's regime, tens of thousands of youths – young men between the ages of eighteen and thirty and considered by the authorities to be the most likely candidates to engage in 'subversive' activities – had been taken from their homes in house-to-house searches and killed. Like other inquirers distanced from the reality of other holocausts, I was aghast and uncomprehend-ing: if people had *known* their houses were going to be searched, why had they not hidden? Why – with sudden inspiration, thinking of the silent, lightweight papyrus boats – had they not gone across the lake at night and hidden out on its wooded islands? Patiently, it was explained to me that if the sons had not been at home when the authorities called, their whole family would have suffered; that they arrived without warning; that if your neighbour was taken, you said to yourself: He must, perhaps, have done something to deserve this – for how else could it be allowed to happen? I recalled the numerous barefoot pedestrians, the roads empty of cars. How far can one flee on foot, alone, in a paranoid country?

The national television had been put to a novel and cathartic use. The survivors, the bereft relatives, the returned exiles, virtually every-one who was willing, had been invited to come forward and tell the country what they had witnessed and suffered.

'Two nights a week,' said Samia, 'you sent your children to bed. You did not eat dinner, but sat with the rest of your family before the television with a bathtowel on your lap, because you knew there would be that much weeping.'

From a cynical point of view, this could be regarded as a clever political ploy by the new government to rally a people, united in their outrage, to its flag. Yet few other possible means of dissipating pain and bitterness so constructively come to mind. Some of the survivors, however, are beyond reconciliation. One of the hotel guests translated for me the speech of a young woman who had returned from exile where she had fled after having been tortured.

'I come back to kill you – and you and you,' she said, pointing to the crowd and the camera. 'You did nothing. Because of *you* I suffered. I have come back to kill you all.'

Bahar Dar, like Gondar, Aksum and Lalibela, had been closed to all visitors for over a year. The few tourists who came to Ethiopia came for 'adventure', and went south to the game parks near the Kenya border and to Omo, where the women wear wooden plates in their lips. With these inescapable facts continually in mind, I found myself, while sitting on the restaurant porch, or on a stone bench by the water, regarding the revived hotel rituals with increasing awe. The bottled water; the coffee and tea served on a little tray with embarrassed apologies for there being no milk; the carefully handwritten daily menu, enclosed in a plastic folder and each day stating that dessert will be 'fresh bananas'; the waiter's dignified walk across the lawn to take an order (more likely from an Ethiopian customer than from a European); the worn, clean tablecloths: how – in an isolated lakeshore town essentially surrounded by villages and bush, amid a population diminished by war and ravaged by grief and dispossession – how is one to regard these proceedings? As ludicrous? Or incalculably heroic?

Lake Tana stands at its elevation of 6000 feet above sea level. From its southern tip the Blue Nile flows forth in a southeasterly direction for some ninety miles before executing a slow curve to the west and then up north into the Sudan. At Khartoum it joins with the White Nile, and for a few months from January onwards, the two rivers flow side by side, their respective currents neither strictly white nor blue, but distinctly discernible none the less. From this point the united rivers are simply 'the Nile'. Between its highland outflowing from Lake

Tana, and the junction at Khartoum, the Blue Nile drops five thousand feet, plunging through gorges so precipitously deep that they were not systematically explored until 1960, when an American survey team sounded their depths using helicopters.

Some seventy miles to the south of Lake Tana, in marshy ground near the village of Sekela, a small and unremarkable stream filters out of the ground and wends its way into the lake. Insignificant as it may appear by virtue of size and the fact that its actual entrance into the vast 1000-square-mile reservoir of Lake Tana makes no visible impression whatsoever, it is held to be the true source of the Blue Nile. This river is called Gishe Abay, or 'the Little Abay', Abay being the indigenous name for what the West has termed the Nile.

The 'discoverer' of the fountains of the Nile in the swampland of Gishe Abay was James Bruce, an aristocratic and wealthy Scotsman who in 1768, at the age of thirty-eight, embarked on his arduous quest for the solution to this most ancient of geographical puzzles. Little was known to the outside world of any of the realms through which Bruce would pass – Sudan, Ethiopia, even Egypt, whose great ancient civilisation had in the eighteenth century yet to be rediscovered. A very few Europeans had penetrated these blank areas of the maps, the most important, for Bruce's story, being the Portuguese Jesuits who had lived and travelled in Ethiopia in the early seventeenth century, and a French doctor named Jacques Poncet who, at the end of the same century, in the capacity of ambassador to the King of France, had accompanied one of the priests as far as Gondar, just above the eastern shore of Lake Tana. The descriptions furnished by these travellers enabled cartographers to chart with general accuracy the location of Lake Tana and the Blue Nile; its relation to the White Nile was of course unknown at this time.

Very little that Bruce had previously achieved could have been considered helpful to the explorer role he assumed. His most important assets appear to have been a facility with languages and an unshakeable self-possession. Six foot four, powerfully built and red-haired, he was a man who would have commanded attention in locales less unlikely than the highlands of Abyssinia. His consciousness of his own worth was very great, and in his eventual five-volume account of his travels he allows himself much scope to assert his character. His style is somewhat Thucydidean in that it is punctuated by purportedly spontaneous speeches of suspect fluency in awkward situations. Arriving in Massawa, the Red Sea port and threshold of Ethiopia, Bruce confronts the sinister Naib (essentially a tribal chief) who has previously threatened him with imprisonment, starvation and death, as well as denying him the authority he seeks to journey inland:

'"Whatever happens to me must befal me in my own house,"' Bruce reports himself as saying. '"Consider what a figure a few naked men will make, the day that my countrymen ask the reason of this either here or in Arabia." I then turned my back, and went out without ceremony. "A brave man!" I heard a voice say behind me. "*Wallah Englese!* True English, by G–d!"'

Bruce eventually made his way to Gondar, at that time the most powerful city in the land, staying at the court of Tecla Haimanout, the fifteen-year-old boy Emperor of Ethiopia. The country was at this time embroiled in a chronic state of petty but savage feuding and tussling for power, and life at court exposed Bruce to some of the more unspeakable after-effects. On the day of his arrival, forty captured rebels had their eyes torn out, before being turned out of the city to meet their fate in the wilderness. One of the King's chief rivals was flayed alive and his skin stuffed and hung from a pole. Even peaceable court life was bloody, and Bruce describes in appalling detail feasts in which the meal's steaks were cut from a living, bellowing cow and eaten raw, while the victim slowly expired at the company's feet. As Alan Moorehead writes in *The Blue Nile*, 'There is an air of nightmarish fantasy about affairs in Ethiopia at this moment.' It is highly probable that one of the incidents Bruce witnessed while in the company of the King (on his return from Gishe Abay) was worked into the final stanzas of 'Kubla Khan':

[The king] had desired me to ride before him, and shew him the horse I had got from Fasil ... It happened that, crossing the deep bed of a brook, a plant of the kantuffa hung across it. I had upon my shoulders a white goat-skin, of which it did not take hold;

but the king, who was dressed in the habit of peace, *his long hair floating all around his face,* wrapt up in his mantle, or thin cotton cloak, *so that nothing but his eyes* could be seen, was paying more attention to the horse than to the branch of kantuffa beside him; it took first hold of his hair, and the fold of the cloak that covered his head ... in such a manner, that ... no remedy remained but he must throw off the upper garment, and appear ... with his head and face bare before all the spectators.

This is accounted a great disgrace to a king, who always appears covered in public ...

With a great show of composure, the King had calmly asked for the 'Shum', the governor of the district. 'Unhappily,' writes Bruce, 'He was not far off':

A thin old man of sixty, and his son about thirty, came trotting, as their custom is, naked to their girdle, and stood before the king ... There is always near the king, when he marches, an officer called Kanitz Kitzera, the executioner of the camp; he has upon the tore of his saddle a quantity of thongs made of bull hide ... this is called the tarade. The king made a sign with his head, and another with his hand, without speaking, and two loops of the tarade were instantly thrown round the Shum and his son's neck, and they were both hoisted upon the same tree, the tarade cut, and the end made fast to a branch. They were both left hanging ...

As Lowes says, this is not the sort of tale one forgets. And in it surely is the inspiration for the lines:

> Beware! Beware!
> His flashing eyes, his floating hair!

Bruce spent eight months at the Gondar court before setting out in October of 1770 for the Nile fountains. His description of the countryside is familiar: there are forests in romantic situations, a grove of magnificent cedars, suggesting a cover for some savage creature. He reminds his companion that the Nile water is enchanted. As they come near to the cliff of Gishe, the ground slopes away in an easy descent, covered all the way with fine grass. Melding with the imagery of the mountains of Kashmir, this is the landscape of Xanadu:

> But oh! that deep romantic chasm which slanted
> Down the green hill athwart a cedarn cover!
> A savage place! as holy and enchanted
> As e'er beneath a waning moon was haunted
> By woman wailing for her demon-lover!

Finally, on 4 November 1770, Bruce reached the elusive fountains, which he first glimpsed, following the direction of his guide's outstretched arm, from a hill on which stood a little church. Throwing off his shoes, Bruce ran down the hill to the edge of the marsh:

> I came after this to the island of green turf, which was in the form of an altar, apparently the work of art, and I stood in rapture over the principal fountain that rises in the middle of it.

Thus in Abyssinia Coleridge discovered yet another 'wilderness-plot, green and fountainous', and moreover in a place savage, holy and romantic.

Two days after our arrival in Bahar Dar, Samia and I waited in the lobby of my hotel for the car, complete with a driver and her two aides, which would take us to Gishe Abay. Samia was wearing a light sweater of silky turquoise cotton over a slim floral skirt, open-toed canvas boat-shoes, and sunglasses. I was aggressively dressed in a long, full, *Out of Africa* skirt, a sensible loose cotton T-shirt, ankle socks (to guard against thorns) and tennis shoes. Caravan Tour and

Travel might be my means of conveyance, but I was, for all that, going to the fountains of the Nile.

The way south to Sekela was over a modestly undulating plain, set against a background of more distant mountains. There were few trees, but the land was otherwise astonishingly lush; green and clipped by grazing, its wide tracks of hoed soil rich brown and moist – in every respect unlike the parched, desolate dustbowl that had been the predominant image of the Ethiopia of my imagination. Although the road took us, naturally enough, through the most inhabited places, the emptiness of this apparently fecund land, the sense of generous space beyond the roadside villages, was striking. One of the policies of the previous government had been the collectivisation of settlements, which entailed the forced abandonment of traditional villages; an incongruous sight were the villages in which remnants of a hammer-and-sickle banner, or stranger yet, the face of Lenin still hung. Another factor accounting for the miles of uninhabited space was that in recent years people had simply fled as far from the roads as they could so as to be out of reach of the factional fighting.

That this road had once been used by troops was apparent from the number of burnt-out or simply abandoned tanks that had been left to rust along the edges; outside one village, they were being used by children as a playground. Several times we were flagged down by strolling soldiers. Our driver hesitated, and then resolutely barrelled on; how seriously does a request for transportation have to be taken, I wondered, when the soldiers are clearly armed?

For many miles beyond Bahar Dar, power lines paralleled the rough road, although the villages we passed were humble and traditional, being conical-roofed dried-mud huts and occasionally cinder-block houses. In spite of the relative dearth of settlements, we passed files of people, the women usually shaven-headed, the men wearing their precarious turbans. The goals of these endless lines of people crisscrossing the plains were the markets that overflowed at various points into the road. Perhaps because so many men and women commonly wore long white cloaks wrapped about them like full-length shawls, banded with red or green and, given the use they were put to, invariably grubby, these markets seemed drab affairs, peopled with indistinct figures carrying wares bound in sacking – a muddle of brown, grey, white and tan so closely pressed together that one could make out neither the goods being sold, nor when a transaction had taken place. The only immediately distinguishable commodities were the chickens, hung live and upside down from carrying sticks, all else being concealed in mysterious bundles.

The appalling simplicity of village life as displayed to the casual observer urges one to search for hidden explanations to justify this bare existence. It cannot simply be that these thin and ragged droves of people are trekking for hours and miles in relentless heat to barter for provisions; it cannot simply be that they are carrying head-loads or driving mule-loads of fuel for their dinner fires; or that the line of barefoot women one passes along the road are out walking for the sole purpose of finding water. Something else, surely, must be taking place beyond the unstinting exercise of these most basic skills of survival; a more elevated explanation must exist and must be sought. Three women appear, the first bearing long shafts of a white fibre, the second carrying a battered umbrella, the third balancing a gourd on her head. One seeks complicated answers when the situation is obvious; one would like to imagine that they are enacting some traditional ceremonial practice, some redemptive ritual. It cannot simply be that they are bringing fire and wood and water to their homes and that the woman who shades herself from the fierce sun does so because she is the only one possessed of an umbrella. Life from the villages overflowed into the road even where there were no markets. A roadside tailor was doing business underneath an umbrella he had strapped to his chair; a man ironed his shirt on the threshold of his hut with an iron hot from the coals in front of his door; a well-dressed cripple crawled on his hands and knees beside the road.

'Are you fond of Strauss?' Samia asked from the back seat behind me. 'I have a tape with me.' We had thus far made our journey to the accompaniment of an assortment of African rock tapes provided by the driver, neither strictly rock nor strictly African. I replied that I did, but this would not make us popular with our companions.

'That is all right,' she said with her winning smile. 'We have supported their music now for some time.'

At the edge of a trim village called Derbete, the road crosses the Little Abay, in this season a substantial russet-coloured river. When the rain comes, it is 'the colour of water', one of Samia's two associates told me. There is in the bare landscape of the plains an air of contentment. The mountains are so far in the distance that they do not present themselves as obstacles or barriers, and one presupposes a way of life that has no need of their protection. The grass seemed now even greener and was embellished by clusters of low-lying yellow flowers. Trees, usually acacia, were still infrequent; of this same area, Bruce had commented that it was in his time being denuded of trees for firewood. Grazing cattle and goats abounded, and the conical huts we passed were neat and looked prosperous, a few of them walled or, less frequently, hedged.

The road skirted a sudden line of hills, and then dipped behind them into a low valley. We continued through this pastoral scenery until the road deposited us at the end of a gentle ascent beside a dark grove of trees walled around with stone. A large, elaborately thatched conical roof could be seen above the trees. This was the roof of St Michael's, the church beside which Bruce had stood to view the Nile fountains.

Banging the van doors behind us, we disembarked, Tecla, Samia's chief aide, commandeering my small day-pack: clearly the order had been given that Madame was to make her explorations unencumbered. A crowd of village children had instantly gathered to form a horseshoe around us, and across the plain and dipping hills herdsmen could also be seen approaching. From Bruce's description, I knew that the Nile fountains lay at the foot of the hill, but my view of them was obscured by a tree nursery down to my left and a small but dense grove of trees directly ahead. Samia explained to the crowd what I wanted, and they nodded approvingly, indicating no surprise at my request. The children scrutinised me thoroughly and seriously, with no childish giggles or squirming; but if any one of us spoke or smiled in their direction, in unison so simultaneous as to appear choreographed, they broke into enormous grins.

As in Bruce's time, the local belief is that Gishe Abay first arises from its underwater course in the depths of mountains some miles hence, but that it breaks into the open only here in the marshy land beside the village. There are two 'fountains', or specific points where the underground water rises, both hard by the grove of trees at the bottom of the hill. One of them, we were told, lay in a 'church', the warden of which would have to be fetched. The sun was high and hard, and Samia produced two small collapsible umbrellas to use as sunshades, and under the shade of these parasols we strolled down the hill escorted by the moving horseshoe of children.

We were soon joined by the warden, who was an old man dressed in tattered trousers: Africa keeps one on one's toes, as a person's importance cannot be reliably judged from his clothes. An arched wooden gate, rather like the entrance to an English country churchyard, opened on to the grove. Across its stone threshold, a short beaten path led through the green light of the trees to a small pond that was enclosed in a kind of bower. Samia had not joined me, but had remained on the threshold talking to the crowd; she was, as I would discover in the course of the experiences we eventually shared, an intensely charismatic person, radiating both authority and a kind of maternal competence that drew people to her. Tecla, however, had come along, both out of curiosity and a concern that I might require something of importance from my rucksack: a notebook and pen, for example, or my hat for the African sun, my sunglasses, my headscarf to be worn as protection from the heat, my camera and extra film, perhaps, or my sunscreen, water bottle, Kleenex, extra socks, or sticking plaster. The pool bottom was dark with leaf mould, but the water itself was cool and clear, as befits a Nile fountain.

Outside again, we proceeded to the second and primary 'source'. Whereas the water in the grove had formed a still pool, that of the second fountain seeped forth in a rivulet whose course could be traced across the plain on the outskirts of the village, very gradually widening and gaining in significance. This, the true source, remains very much as Bruce described it – a dark hole in the middle of a small hillock of sodden turf enclosed by a double ring of small stones, which Bruce termed an altar. If one stamps the ground from the edge of the marsh, the small dark hole of water shakes, as if the whole hill were floating on a river.

The impressive crowd now gathered of men and children – no women – watched me fixedly as I made my way towards the circle of stones. I had taken off my shoes so as not to get them wet, and this too they had watched with intense interest. Samia asked if I wanted a photograph taken – well, why not? – and I assented. The children were extraordinarily well-mannered, scuttling aside so as not to spoil the picture, but beaming delightedly if asked to pose.

At the end of our excursion, we returned to look at the church, which stood in its overgrown stone-walled enclosure. Architecturally, it derived from the humble village hut, being a mud-brick rondavel covered with a thatched conical roof, but its size and the intricacy of its thatching made it a commanding structure. It was firmly locked up behind closed wooden doors and shutters which, together with the untended grass, suggested that the church was defunct; I was assured, however, that it was opened regularly for services. There are a great many of these distinctive churches throughout the country – the islands and peninsulas of Lake Tana are particularly noteworthy in this respect – often containing brilliant, striking frescoed walls, which may date back centuries, a testimony to the vigilant maintenance on the part of the priests.

A still larger crowd had congregated to observe my perambulations around the church and its yard, and when I came to leave, many people stepped forward to smile and shake my hand and wish me a good journey. On the return trip, we stopped to have a late afternoon picnic that Samia had prepared, sitting at leisure on fine grass in the shade of a wild orchard of low, twisted trees.

'This part of the country is beautiful,' remarked Samia. 'But it is a shame. I do not think I could take a tour here. Three hours out, and three hours back – it is a long time for most tourists to see so little. They are not like you, who loves to see beautiful Nature.'

As we approached Bahar Dar, the driver and Tecla began to laugh amongst themselves, and Samia turned to me to translate.

'They are saying the people of the village are so superstitious. As you were leaving, the people were saying that they could no longer use their water.'

I looked puzzled.

'Yes. They believe, Caroline, that their water is holy, and that a woman's touch will defile it. Many people come to the water to get healed; but now,' she laughed, 'they say it will not work.'

With dawning comprehension, I recalled how Samia herself had always stood back on the perimeter.

'No,' she replied to my question, 'they would never have let me enter. But you were a visitor.'

This incident was to me emblematic of Africa's at once great strength and great weakness; its people would endure to see their holy places trodden underfoot, rather than be impolite to a stranger. It was too late to turn back and tell the villagers I had not known.

In Addis, where I was to spend a few days before departing for Dessie, the rain was harder and heavier than before I had left for Bahar Dar. The unpaved roads were swimming in mud, and those that were paved seemed on the verge of cracking open. People walked resolutely bare-headed through the rain, or stood flattened against buildings and trees in an attempt to stay dry.

Back in the Ghion Hotel, I attempted to get tea and something to eat at teatime, but the coffee-shop, bar, lobby, restaurant and room service were either closed or otherwise engaged, and I left for my room discouraged. Some hours later, however, as I was going out for dinner, I was accosted by the young woman who ran a small business centre within the hotel.

'I have heard you were looking everywhere for tea,' she told me urgently. 'Please, next time come to me. I am always here, and I can give you tea *and* cake.'

Early on the morning of departure for Gishen Mariam, Samia arrived at the Ghion Hotel with the jeep and driver she had 'organised'. The plan had been that we would drop her off at her home, before setting out for Dessie. I was, therefore, somewhat confused when we drove out of the city limits and I saw that the driver gave no indication that he intended to stop any time soon. Concerned, I turned to ask if we had overshot a turn-off.

Samia's eyes were brilliant. 'I cannot help it! I have to come with you! I couldn't sleep all last night, and my husband said – Samia, you must finish your adventure!'

My impression from the air on arrival in Ethiopia had been of a barren land of almost biblical character, a terraced palette of brown hues ranging from mahogany to sable that appeared to have the gently nubbed texture of worn felt. One did not imagine that this land was overgrazed, which admitted the unthinkable possibility that it had previously been green; rather, one accepted it as a specific form of terrain whose nature did not permit growth of any kind. In other aerial overviews of parched lands, I have gained a sense of settled, if beaten, communities, but the biblical aspect of my first glimpse of Ethiopia had arisen from the impression it gave of being conducive only to nomads, to restless, weary, uprooted wandering in search of a place in which life of any kind might conceivably be supported. Once on the ground, this impression is both contradicted and substantiated, depending upon what region one visits, and at what time of year. The land around Lake Tana, for example, had clearly belied this. But the harsh, rugged mountainscape in which Gishen Mariam lay seemed to have been fashioned expressly to test the limits of human endurance.

The countryside immediately outside Addis was dramatically mountainous and, under the lifeless sky of this early rainy season, sombre. Apart from clumps of wind-blown blue-gum trees, the land that rolled away on either side of the road was as featureless as a prairie, and astonishingly extensively cultivated. Dark brown acre upon acre of meticulously turned soil, but only a handful of huts were passed – where was the workforce that had so painstakingly transformed so many miles? The vast majority of Ethiopia's estimated population of over fifty million live in rural areas, while four-fifths of the workforce are engaged in mostly subsistence agriculture. But again, the recent wars had driven many of the people away from roads and to safer, less accessible areas.

Gradually the arable land gave way to more rugged terrain, and about eighty miles outside the capital the road tunnelled through a sheer cliff, emerging on the other side to overlook a spectacular and unexpectedly luxuriant upland valley, whose terraced slopes and floor were patchworked with the colours of its various crops and fields. Here the air was bluff and cool, with clean vistas over the valley; but after some hours of descent we found ourselves crawling across the floor of a murderously hot valley of a very different nature, whose naked walls were crumbling and powdery, the leaves of all its trees wilting, and where even the desert-hardy aloes had dried out, uprooted and keeled over. The desiccated bush sang like a live wire with cicadas.

Streams of people appeared, more than we had seen in one place anywhere else, walking barefoot on the tarmac road, or, if they were children, skipping and running and waving at us as we passed. Every male, of whatever age, was possessed of a long stick, which he walked with, carried over his shoulders, used to herd animals, or propped himself on when standing. The young girls were strikingly beautiful, with their hair worn in thick, glossy shoulder-length braids that streamed behind them as they ran, and with large silver medallions flashing from their necks. But for all the life and energy exhibited, one was indignant for them – why live here, when only miles away there lay lush highlands?

The huts one saw now were not even shacks, but haystacks, slipping piles of straw into which human beings burrowed to eat and sleep. Further still, and I noted with a kind of horror that the dry cliff-face abutting the road had been terraced for crops. As if by way of a definitive statement that we had entered a different land, two camels sauntered out of the scrub and ambled down the road, unattended. There was a glint and shimmer from the river flood-plain that paralleled the road, not of water, for the river-bed was dry, but the reflection of rocks under the bare sun. Later, we came upon a knot of people washing and sitting like blissful hippos in a thin, terrible trickle that had somehow appeared among the parched river stones. By imperceptible degrees, this stream must have gained strength, for further yet, and suddenly the valley floor was again transformed, the flood-plain now green and grazed by numerous cattle, watered by real rivers – and one's very soul drew a deep sigh of relief.

The town of Dessie made its first appearance as a ramshackle congestion of huts and houses slipping down the sides of a mountain. Within the town, narrow pot-holed streets led the way between lines of crooked buildings valiantly painted in cheerful colours – green, turquoise, pink – beneath their battered roofs. One felt that some deep force underlying the whole range of encircling mountains had recently shrugged, and sent a ripple of disturbance through the whole town that had made it slightly cockeyed. Balconies and terraces slanted dangerously and whole buildings were askew.

A number of signs indicated the presence of relief organisations. Between 1984 and 1985, Dessie was the site of one of the most desperate droughts and famines to inflict the country in a century. In 1984, seven million Ethiopians faced starvation, by outside reckoning, principally in the northernmost provinces of Tigré, Eritrea and Wollo, of which Dessie is the regional capital. The causes of this disaster were man-made as well as natural. The northern provinces have historically been so over-cultivated that the fertility of the soil has been depleted, and deforestation and loss of vegetation coverage so drastic as to produce a climactic change – the annual precipitation in these regions is calculated as being less than one-half of what it was ten years ago, a fact attributed by environmentalists to the loss of oxygen-producing greenery.

Coupled with this were the disastrous 'reforms' mandated by the previous government, such as the collectivisation of villages in conformity with socialist practice. A second human contribution was more sinister. The hundreds of thousands of tons of grain that had been airlifted from nations around the world were denied immediate delivery – and sometimes delivery at all – to the most desperate areas. Supplies were diverted to pay off army troops and into the hands of high-up government and military officials, who could later profit by their resale. It is the belief of many people in the country that the ongoing border hostilities between Ethiopia and Somalia, which together with the internal disputes with the northern provinces resulted in displacing two million refugees, had been deliberately exacerbated by the Ethiopian government so as to distract the attention of the world community from its domestic wars. Although there is currently no famine in Ethiopia, the afflicted regions had not recovered from their recent tribulation, which upset the traditional rhythm of food production and brought on its heels livestock and agricultural diseases.

Samia and I checked into Dessie's cheerless government-owned hotel. The dust from the road had made us both several shades darker than our respective natural colours, but there was no running water available, and we had to make do with bucket showers.

In the middle of the night, I awoke to hear distant gunfire, and at breakfast the next morning asked Samia about it.

'Yes, I heard it too. But the weapons, they were not very modern.' She laughed. 'You see – we have all become arms experts over the years.' In Addis, there had been long periods in which gunfire had been part of the fabric of daily life. During one grim period, city residents on their way to work in the morning had confronted the victims of the night before laid out in the streets with warning signs nailed to their corpses.

After breakfast, the driver, who had stayed with relatives, took Samia, me and a local friend of Samia's named Esewbalu, to the market in order to buy food for the long journey to Gishen Mariam. Esewbalu was an earnest, pleasant young man who worked for the Ministry of Sports and Culture, and who had taught himself English, as so many young people in Africa do, primarily by listening to English-language radio. The market here at least was well supplied, with papaya, sugar cane, bags of herbs, potatoes and chickens ferried in and out by bellowing camels and heavily laden women. Our driver was a small, dainty-featured man, who maintained throughout the hours of arduous driving a serene and distant smile. Although he clearly understood Samia and me when we spoke in English, he himself said very little. Now, however, seeing that I was intrigued with the market, he volunteered his observations, at the same time revealing that there are learning fonts of English other than *Voice of America*.

'You notice it is crowded?' he asked. 'Many people have come here because of the Relief. There is no work, and many people are filling the town. There are loiterers. There are thieves, vagabonds and brigands.'

Gishen Mariam, high in the Ambasel range, is by map only forty or so miles north of Dessie, but was a drive that would demand five hours in either direction, due to the brutally rugged condition of the untreated road. The monastic tradition in Ethiopia is ancient and widespread, dating from the fifth century, when it was said to have been introduced by Syrian monks. Under Haile Selassie, the Ethiopian Orthodox Church was decreed to be the state religion, a position that it lost under the Marxist regime. Although Gishen Mariam is still today the focus of an annual pilgrimage, it is by no means one of the better-known monastic sites. The legendary rock-hewn church of remote Lalibela, dating from the twelfth century, is probably the most famous; the most intriguing may be St Mary's Church at Aksum, which claims possession of the original Ark of the Covenant, said to have been taken out of Israel in the tenth century BC by Menelik I, the son of Solomon and the founder of the Ethiopian royal line. From everything I had heard and read, the modern priesthood, which was particularly strong in the countryside, represented an ancient, venerable and well-schooled tradition, which had successfully safeguarded its church's lore and musical and liturgical practices throughout centuries of tribulations. The priests are regarded as prophets with honour in their own country, where there are today eighteen-and-a-half million people of the Ethiopian Orthodox faith.

A north-going road from Dessie led us into a worn-out valley etched by the rocky bed of what in another season might be a river. This, at a strategic point, we lurched across, picking up the single road on the opposite bank, which crawled around the crumbling mountains. Road, river, mountains – all were the colour of sand. Here and there in the river-bed one could spy pools of rushes or greenery, but elsewhere only scraps of herbage survived loosely rooted in the soil. An hour or so out on the mountain road, we found the way blocked by a giant cactus tree that had fallen from the over-hanging cliff. Disembarking from the jeep, we began to dismember it, pulling its spongy limbs away after only a few chops of a machete. Surprisingly, the sun, which was high and direct, was not unduly hot, and a vigorous wind blew past the mountain and down the valley.

So far, since leaving Dessie we had passed only a scattering of huts, usually standing just below the road, with the tips of their conical, thatched roofs protruding above it. Now, a man and a young boy appeared in the dust, dressed in rags and walking heavily under head-loads of wood. Seeing us, they stopped and unloaded, and with scarcely a word exchanged began hacking at the tree with their knives. Samia and I, as the patrons of the journey, were waved aside, and Esewbalu, presumably as an educated man and therefore unworthy of manual labour, withdrew himself, and so we stood to-gether, uselessly regarding the proceedings. The young boy, at nearly six feet, was strikingly tall for his age, and had seemed slender as he approached us on the road. Now I observed with a shock that his long legs did not vary in width – that from ankle to upper thigh, they were no thicker than my fist. The picture of undernourishment that I carried in my mind had principally been derived from media coverage of relief centres showing listless, patient men and women sitting dully in sand-blown tents. It was a shock to see that, on the contrary, the chronically underfed do not always sit and languish, but must work and walk and carry loads and carry life ahead. When the tree had been successfully dragged out of the way, our two vol-unteers turned immediately to their head-loads and started on their way – they had expected neither a ride, nor payment, and we had to chase after them and call them back.

Somewhat further, and we came to a solitary branch in the road marked by a dented sign bearing the words 'Gishen Mariam', in Amharic and Roman letters, and an arrow pointing up the higher track. From this juncture to just below the summit where we parked, the road was almost unnegotiable, steeply angled and drifted with rocky landfall, and on more than one occasion we had to get out and walk behind the grinding jeep. Unfolding below us, as we rounded each progressively higher curve, was a vast plain pillared with flat-topped massifs, each so regularly etched with identical lines of sedimentation as to have clearly belonged, in ages past, to a single all-encompassing tableland. Disconcertingly, as if the disparate bluffs had only moments before been rent asunder, the mind's eye strove to piece them back into their proper unity.

We rounded another bend, and in the distance above I saw what could at first glance be taken for a man-made fortress, a mountain whose blunt panoramic summit was rimmed with a peculiar stratification of rock that lent it the appearance of an encircling battlement. Of all the mountains on the plain, I felt this had to be Mount Abora.

Our spiral up the mountain ended with the road beside a group of huts situated on a small, level bluff. Worn in the rock-face to our left, a narrow path, like a goat trail, zigzagged a short distance up the mountain, where it intersected a giddying flight of rock-cut steps. Surmounting these were the iron gates that guarded the only entrance to the citadel, imposing and fringed overhead by tassels made of tin that fluttered and rang like flimsy bells in the raking wind. A white-robed gatekeeper bowed elaborately as we passed, his outstretched arm sweeping us on to the platform of the summit.

The mountain takes the form of a rough cross, and we had entered on to one of its transepts. A lean-to hut and bare flagpole were the only outstanding objects on the barren rock plateau, but further on we confronted another, shorter flight of steps running beside a thatch-topped retaining wall, which half hid a group of huts. A line of curious children trickled out to watch as we approached a church enclosure which appeared directly ahead of us, but at the sound of a woman's angry voice from one of the huts, they vanished behind their wall again.

Kidrai Maryam, or the Church of Holy Mary, was an octagonal stone building capped by a swooping conical tin roof, and cheerfully embellished by a colonnade of pale blue pillars, towering red wooden doors, double-arched windows and crocus-yellow walls. A young boy who had trailed behind us into the churchyard volunteered that the church was kept shut, but that he would fetch the priests to let us in. After he had darted off, we settled on the church steps and enjoyed the calm of the enclosure, which was set within a grove of blue-gums, and encircled with juniper. The wind, the tintinnabulation of the tinny fringe and one lone bird were the only sounds to be heard.

A new messenger arrived shortly to tell us that the priests would meet us at yet another church that lay near by, and obediently we rose and followed our guide. The second church proved to be an unexpected sight, being shaped like an oversized barrel with tubby transepts, painted brilliant white and decorated with crimson and gilt arabesques, paisleys and other florid motifs unambiguously borrowed from the Muslim world. Crowning this phenomenon was a handsome conical tin roof surmounted by an ornate cross that resembled a giant Christmas snowflake. Set as it was on this remote mountain summit in a desolate plain, in an area elsewhere reeking of poverty, it was a resplendent if incongruous apparition.

The small crowd that had drifted into the enclosure to watch us now became very agitated, beginning to bow and genuflect in anticipation of the priests, who, sure enough, soon appeared led by the abbot himself, a handsome, bearded patriarch, wearing over his slacks and tennis shoes a white robe that swirled in the wind. The lesser priests behind him were scrappier versions of the abbot, thinner, scantier of beard and clad in grubby robes, and who on catching up with the abbot began an elaborate ceremony of reverential greeting, although they had essentially arrived together. The abbot received his acolytes in a manner befitting a pope, gazing into the distance while each priest bowed before him and ritualistically kissed a heavy iron cross that he apparently carried for this sole purpose. First the forehead, then the lips were touched with the cross, which was next reversed with a practised flip of the abbot's wrist, then the lips again. Forehead, lips (flip), lips; forehead, lips (flip), lips. The abbot was adept enough to conduct this rite while looking skyward with an abstracted air. When the priests had been dealt with, a few of the bold ventured forward from the watchful bobbing crowd to receive the cross themselves, and a couple of little boys approached the church to prostrate themselves on its threshold, kissing the steps and then the lintels. Finally, everyone was finished, and the priests and abbot looked around and rested their attention on us.

Samia and I greeted the abbot with respectful bows, and Samia
explained that we wished to see inside the church. The abbot replied
that this was the church under whose floor was guarded the True
Cross of the Crucifixion, and that no women were allowed inside, a
pronouncement that was not entirely unexpected, this being the
practice of many of the churches in the country. I now noticed that
there were no women, or even little girls, among the people who had
gathered to watch our reception.

'Oh well,' I said, resignedly.

'Go closer, Caroline,' said my trusty guide.

I stepped tentatively towards the church.

'You can go closer,' Samia directed. The abbot, however, called
out to her.

'He is saying that you must stop at the stones,' said Samia, referring
to three large blocks that formed a kind of altar. 'But pretend you do
not understand. Go closer.'

I stopped uncertainly by the altar.

'Closer, Caroline,' said Samia, as the priests called out again, and
began to address her excitedly.

Samia giggled. 'These priests say that last year two women tried to
enter the church. One became a stone statue, and the other fell into a
hole that opened at her feet.' Samia turned back to the priests, and
then reported to me.

'I asked them how could that be? Before they arrived, we ate our
picnic here on the church steps and nothing happened. Go closer,
Caroline.'

I stepped past the altar, and the abbot intervened.

'He says you can go a few steps past the altar. Closer, Caroline.'
Behind me, more words followed, but I sensed, without looking, that
a tide of sorts had turned. Samia was interrogating, and the priests
were confusedly answering.

'I have told them that you have travelled thousands of miles to
write about our country, and that you will tell the world that in
Ethiopia, the priests keep their churches locked to the people. In
addition, their road here is in terrible condition. Closer, Caroline.'

Behind me, a directive must have been given, for a priest strode past me to the church, unlocked the doors and threw them open, and then vanished into the shadows of the interior. Moments later, a sudden flare of light revealed him standing to one side of the door holding a flaming taper above his head. Dimly, I could make out a patterned backdrop of some kind.

'I have told them you need to take pictures,' Samia called. 'Go closer, Caroline, pretend you cannot see.'

I edged my way uneasily forward, waving my camera. I could now make out a large drum lying on its side on a carpeted floor. More words had been exchanged behind my back, and Samia called out that I should ascend the steps to the threshold, which I did, with no comments at all from the priests.

'All the way to the top step, Caroline. Can you see what you want, or should we get you inside?'

In fact, I could see all that I needed to. The back wall was hung with European religious pictures of a sentimental nature flanked by worn floral curtains, which the taper-bearing priest had pulled aside for my inspection. According to tradition, it was under this inner shrine that part of the holy cross, brought from Jerusalem in the late fourteenth century, is safeguarded: other scholars might speculate that the tradition of the church arose from the rough cruciform nature of the *amba*.

Of the estimated two hundred individuals residing on Gishen Mariam, seventy-two were priests. With few exceptions, all were locally trained, meaning they had essentially lived their lives on Gishen Mariam's summit. 'Priest', it soon transpired, was a kind of codeword for 'adult male resident', all males on the mountain belonging to this brotherhood.

'What do you want to be when you grow up?' I asked Samia and Esewbalu to inquire of a knot of children who followed us around the *amba*.

'Priests,' said the little boys, one and all. But the little girls said nothing.

'What about a pilot? What about a doctor?' Esewbalu asked them.

'What's a pilot? What's a doctor?' they answered. The priests are apparently not required to abstain from pleasures of the flesh, and so most of the children on the mountain are their own offspring. The boys, on attaining manhood, will be inducted by their older brothers, and taught the priestly ritual secrets, such as opening the church each morning, sweeping it out, kissing the cross, beating the ritual drums, and chanting the liturgy. They do not necessarily have to learn to read and write, and there are no schools on the mountain. The girls, on attaining womanhood, essentially become the servants of the men – increasing the duties they have previously carried out – and produce more priests.

'And why not be a priest?' as Samia said. 'And why not be treated like a king?'

The physical structure of many of these monastic churches – a rondavel with a narrow interior peristyle encircling the sanctum sanctorum – essentially precludes interior congregational services. Groups of worshippers of any size must be preached to outside, thus ensuring that the churches remain the exclusive domain of the priests. The churches are in any case kept locked throughout the day and night, and normally opened only for cleaning in the morning, 'when the people are away', as the abbot said. There are currently three churches on the mountain, and a fourth is in the process of being built.

'Why do you not build schools? Why do you have no clinic?' Samia scolded the abbot.

'The people want churches,' the patriarch replied with dignity.

Ethiopian Orthodox services incorporate a great deal of music and drumming in their liturgy, an aspect of worship that has its roots in the Old Testament. Gishen Mariam caters to its largest crowd at *Maskal*, an annual festival celebrating the original discovery of the cross in AD 326 by the Empress Helena, and an occasion that attracts hundreds of gift-bearing pilgrims. The pilgrimage offerings were stored in a 'museum' near the church, to which we were led by a bleary-eyed priest, redolent of beer.

At the top of a flight of shaky wooden steps, a door opened on to a kind of loft, filled with neatly folded and piled-up rugs, row upon row of ornate prayer umbrellas and, as in an opera chorus's changing room, a rack of sumptuous silk and lace cassocks. A shelf of dusty leatherbound books – sacred texts – stood to one side, while in pride of place at the centre were stacked religious icons apparently culled from gift shops in holy places around the world, whose treasures included metallic wall clocks depicting the Last Supper, doormats woven with the face of the Mother of God, posters and other religious curios.

'Cultural history,' Esewbalu whispered, lowering his voice as in a church. During our interview with the abbot, he had busily applied himself to transcribing the holy man's *ipsissima verba* as they fell from his lips. The pilgrim offerings provide the priests with their livelihood, our guide explained, and from time to time choice gifts are selected for sale down the mountain.

On leaving, I complimented the priest on the beauty of his church, noting its unusual façade. He looked pleased and nodded, explaining that a hundred years or so ago, in the time of Menelik II, one of the priests had been abroad and seen the gorgeous decorations on the mosques, and subsequently arranged to procure two Arabic craftsmen to decorate the newly built church. When, after several years, they had completed their work, the priests took them aside and chopped off their hands, for as infidels, they could not be allowed to walk away free after laying their hands on the church of the True Cross. This story, whether true or not, may also reflect the tradition, reported by a sixteenth-century traveller, that any stranger attempting to enter the royal citadel of Mount Amara was punished by having his eyes put out and his hands and feet cut off.

In the early evening, we made our way back down the mountain, the driver carefully carrying a bottle of dirty water and some soil that the priests had blessed and sold to him. The wind had become stronger as the day wore on, and the tin tassels above the summit gateway were jangling frenetically. Beyond the gates, we met on the narrow rock steps an old woman bent so low under her back-load of wood that her elbows almost touched the ground. Her eyes were staring and she was gulping for breath.

'Take your time, mother,' said Esewbalu, as she tried to step aside for us. 'We will pass when you are ready.'

'You are kind, you are kind,' she replied, leaning heavily against the rock balustrade.

'You have come far, mother,' said Samia.

'Yes,' she replied. 'It would not be so bad, if there were only water at the top.'

'If the priests had to carry their own wood and water, I do not think they would live so high on the mountain,' said Samia, when the woman had lurched past.

We had left our departure too late. The valley, at a thousand feet below, so steep that its floor had earlier been lost in its own shadow, was now wrapped in a dull haze, behind which the sun was already slipping. It was well into night when we arrived in Dessie, our valiant driver having had to negotiate the treacherous return journey more or less in the dark.

'The way was long and dangerous,' he summarised, turning off the ignition. 'But we are all happy. Everything on the programme was a success.'

James Bruce returned to England in 1774, six years after his departure for Africa, with the expectation of a hero's welcome and a possible baronetcy from King George III. In Paris, where he had dallied for some time before coming to London, the story of his travels and his bulky portfolio of sketches, botanical specimens, linguistic studies, charts and anthropological observations were received with much acclaim. But a very different reception awaited him in London.

Of Bruce's many foreign accomplishments, the one that in his own eyes justified and outshone all else was, of course, his discovery of the fountains of the Nile. But, as it happened, in 1618, approximately a hundred and fifty years before James Bruce, a Portuguese priest named Father Paez had visited many of the places in Abyssinia recorded by Bruce, including that unprepossessing patch of marshy land hard by Sekela. A description of this site, moreover, was published some twelve years later in 1630, by a fellow Jesuit, Father Jeronimo Lobo; it is unclear whether Lobo himself also visited the fountains, or merely based his written account on Paez's manuscript.

In either case, Father Lobo's work, which overtly refers to Paez, was available to Bruce in English. Some forty years before Bruce's reappearance on the London scene, a translation had been made of Lobo's book from a French copy of the lost Portuguese original, entitled *A Voyage to Abyssinia*; and it was Bruce's ill fate that this translation had been made by none other than Dr Samuel Johnson, author of *The History of Rasselas, Prince of Abissinia*, and regarded as the authority on things Abyssinian, as on all else. Johnson's preface to the translation was, moreover, when read in the light of objections that would be made to Bruce's extraordinary claims, presciently pointed:

> The Portuguese Traveller [Johnson had written in 1735] contrary to the general Vein of his Countrymen, has amused his Reader with no Romantick Absurdities or Incredible Fictions ... He appears, by his modest and unaffected Narrative to have described Things as he saw them, to have copied Nature from the Life, and to have consulted his Senses not his Imagination; He meets with no Basilisks that destroy with their Eyes, his Crocodiles devour their Prey without Tears, and his Cataracts fall from the Rock without Deafening the Neighbouring Inhabitants.

Johnson's view of Bruce was that a man whose major claim to attention was manifestly founded on falsehood deserved little sympathetic hearing in anything else, a pronouncement that served to vindicate the prevailing opinion in London that Bruce was a teller of romantic tales. A supplement to the comic story of the extravagant 'travels' of the fictive Baron Münchhausen was published and 'humbly dedicated to Mr Bruce the Abyssinian traveller'. The charge was even made that Bruce had never set foot in Africa, but had hidden out in Armenia for all the years of his absence. Bruce's claim to have discovered an ancient painting of an Egyptian harp in a rock tomb in Medidnet Habu was singled out for special ridicule, largely on account of its popular conflation with his dissertations on Abyssinian musical instruments and on an unkind pun of 'liar' for 'lyre'. Egyptian harps, Abyssinian lyres – somewhere in this soup of associations surely lies the inspiration for the Abyssinian maid with a dulcimer in the final, 'Ethiopian' stanza of 'Kubla Khan'.

In disappointment, disgust and bitterness, Bruce withdrew to Scotland. He married, occupied himself with his estate and locked away his voluminous Ethiopian material. In 1785, his beloved wife died, and it was perhaps this loss, which he felt keenly, that eventually rekindled a concern for his reputation and honour. At any rate, it was not long afterwards that Bruce turned his attention back to his old journals, and embarked on the writing of a memoir of his Abyssinian experience. Although he had notebooks, letters, charts and logbooks to work from, he preferred to work – at this distance of so many years – from his memory; and moreover, in preference to doing the writing himself, he chose to dictate to an assistant who struggled to keep pace with his flow of words. Unhappily for Bruce, the publication of *Travels to Discover the Source of the Nile*, in 1790, only succeeded in reawakening the ridicule of the years before.

'The world makes a strange mistake when it supposes that I would condescend to write a romance for its amusement,' Bruce is reported to have said to his daughter. In his lifetime, he never received the vindication he desired and deserved, and to the end of his life he was held to be something of an eccentric. After his death in 1794, however, little by little, different aspects of his account were confirmed by scholars and explorers. And in the early nineteenth century, in the rock tomb of Rameses III at Medidnet Habu was found a delicate painting of an Egyptian harp – and Bruce's name scratched on the rock surface beside it.

Coleridge, in a passage of one of his more discursive late writings that could have been modelled on Bruce's story, tells a parable about 'a poor pilgrim benighted in a wilderness or desert, and pursuing his way in the starless dark with a lantern in his hand'. By happy chance, the pilgrim stumbles on an oasis of surpassing beauty. 'Deep, vivid, and faithful are the impressions, which the lovely imagery comprised within the scanty circle of light makes and leaves on his memory'.

Frightened by a noise, the pilgrim hurries forward: and as he passes with hasty steps through grove and glade, shadows and imperfect beholdings and vivid fragments of things distinctly seen blend with the past and present shapings of his brain. Fancy modifies sight. His dreams transfer their forms to real objects . . . and when at a distance from this enchanted land, and on a different track, the dawn of day discloses to him a caravan, a troop of his fellow-men, his memory, which is itself half fancy, is interpolated afresh by every attempt to recall, connect, and piece out his recollections. His narration is received as a madman's tale. He shrinks from the rude laugh and contemptuous sneer, and retires into himself.

There are few better examples than James Bruce to illustrate the difficulties inherent in attempting to revive the symphony and song of an experience. Bruce's adventures, generally, were confirmed; but much could – and has – been said of the manner in which he rendered his personal account. Bruce himself had been well aware of the earlier journey of the Portuguese priests, but his zeal for his quest, his desire to distinguish himself in some great way, his vanity, and his morbid hatred of Catholicism conspired to blind him, one feels genuinely so, to their prior claim. His description of Tissisat Falls, the Blue Nile's first major cataract, is entirely, perversely flavoured by his determination not to see it as his Jesuit predecessors described it. And at Khartoum, where the Blue and White Nile join forces, how could he have avoided the apprehension that there was 'another Nile', and consequently another fountain that had yet to be discovered?

All of these shortcomings serve to indicate the extreme difficulty of making objective observations in the first place, and of recalling them objectively in the second. These problems are compounded when attempting to recreate in writing a journey one has undertaken. Like most genres of literature, travel narration is determined, if not to a great degree defined, by conventional dictates. Bruce's extraordinary account of his extraordinary journey has, it will be recalled, been termed 'the epic of African travel'. All epics require a hero; specifically, they require a single hero, which assuredly accounts for the reason why the European companion of Bruce's adventures – the gifted young Italian architect and draughtsman Luigi Balugani, who was present throughout the major part of Bruce's travels, and in particular when Bruce ran down the grassy hill at Gishe Abay – has been completely and utterly expunged from Bruce's story.

Early in the diaries of my own Ethiopian travels, a certain restless dissatisfaction can be detected. 'A pleasantly useless day,' I wrote shortly after my arrival in Addis, at the exact point at which I had finally solved the transportation dilemma, and knew that my trip was in good order. Why, one has to wonder, 'useless'? Had I not systematically made my way to all the 'must see' spots? Had I not met numerous informative and charming people and – the desideratum of all travellers – even had meals in their homes? ('You can't get food in the restaurants. For *real* Ethiopian food you have to go their houses.') With hindsight and more self-awareness, I recognise now the source of my discontent. It was not only that things were being organised for me, and I was feeling – and existing – like a tourist, but, more dangerously, in Samia Kebire I had discovered a personality so dynamic, so efficient, so full of good sense and fun, that I recognised that if she accompanied me on the Blue Nile journey, I could no longer be the hero of my own story.

Traditionally, travel narrative is an inherently romantic genre, in the original and strictest sense of the word, which was coined in the mid-seventeenth century when French heroic and medieval romances had widespread popularity in England. 'Romantic' meant, literally, 'like the romances', which were in turn characterised by 'improbable adventures remote from ordinary life'. Invariably, in the course of a journey one will encounter situations that, gratifyingly, fall within the compass of this definition; but, increasingly, many events and situations will not, as the realities of modern travel cannot be relied upon to yield experiences that meet the old romantic expectations. The temptation is very great, therefore, when playing the hero of one's own story, to dismiss and edit away all incidents that do not fit the traditional mould. All good travel narratives feature a trusty native guide; but he should be dressed in flamboyant traditional robes or, alternatively, in rags, and it is distracting if this guide is a chic, sophisticated woman; and it is downright jarring if the guide is unabashedly a tourist agent. Being the hero of a travel story has historically presupposed a cultural superiority to the country visited and a global access denied indigenous people; but now when the distant traveller arrives in Prester John's kingdom, he may find that, courtesy of CNN, much about him and his world is already known.

Most seriously, 'development', whatever else it may be, is not romantic; and one does not read travel literature simply in order to relive the familiar and mundane experiences of one's own 'world' in an unfamiliar setting: all the talk at the beginning of this chapter about how difficult it was to find a car, about the wretched hotel, the flight to Bahar Dar – who hasn't flown in bad weather? No, let our hero set out from a tent or mud hut or pasha's court, and spare the reader these tedious details.

Neither the world, nor our perception of it, has yet changed so much since Bruce's time that romantic stories cannot still be written. The ingredients are usually there in most travel 'experiences' and only require judicious editing. Certainly, I could have given a more ... palatable account of a journey to the fountains of the Nile. There had been some instances of sniper activity, for example, and these dangers I could surely have played up. I could have skipped the plane ride altogether and simply 'arrived' in Bahar Dar. The Ghion Hotel on Lake Tana's shores, with its flocks of kingfishers, herons, fish eagles and iridescent starlings, with its frangipani, jacaranda, hibiscus and magnificent strangling fig could surely have been made more exotic. 'Native' life in the roadside villages could have been made to seem either more savage, or more mysterious; and I could have referred to my driver, but made no mention of my guide. If really desperate, it is of course possible to contrive difficulties. I could have insisted on hiring a mule for the last mile of the journey or, alternatively, made my trip deep into the rainy season when I would have had to do so. I could have sought out the worst possible lodgings, and then dwelt on my discomfort. In short, while the old epics belong to an age when the world was glamorously inaccessible, an acceptable, modern, mini-epic could still have been devised. The question is, can one in good faith deny a country its painfully acquired progressions? Can one's experience of a country be tailored to the exigencies of one's own romantic quest?

The modern traveller will inevitably find himself walking self-consciously in the footsteps of an earlier, more illustrious predecessor, compared to whose adventures his own may seem prosaic and dull. Yet, for all that, even in an age when it is possible to take a day trip to the fountains of the Nile, I do not believe that making journeys to regions remote from one's ordinary life will cease to allure and fascinate. I do believe, however, that it will become increasingly difficult for the traveller to cut the dashing figure of the old romantic epics; or, like Bruce, to pretend to himself that he has done so.

Ethiopia was the last of my destinations. My travels had awarded me glimpses – albeit scattered – of the landscape of Xanadu. Now, nothing remained for me but to turn to the place where it had been conjured up and to the poet who had dreamed it.

EXMOOR

Exmoor

Early in the year 1797, Coleridge established himself and his small household in Nether Stowey, a village at the foot of the picturesque Quantock Hills on the southwest coast of England. His fantasy of a pantisocratic existence had by this time been abandoned, but it was his hope that in the isolation of the Somerset–Devon borderland he would be able to replicate something of the essence of his Utopian dream without a company of comrades. The move to Stowey also amounted to a renouncement of the other possible pursuits with which he had previously toyed, such as teaching and practising as a dissenting preacher, in favour of a serious and single-minded dedication to his writing. His first child, Hartley, had been born in September of the preceding year, and this event seems to have acted as a strong inducement for him to rethink and refocus his life.

Financial realities, an uncomfortably small and ill-furnished house and the dawning awareness that his passive wife, Sara, was not the perfect mate were a few of the concerns that prevented the actualisation of Coleridge's dream of rustic tranquillity and productivity. His literary output was for the most part fragmentary. On the other hand, as part of his poetic master plan, he was reading voraciously.

'I should not think of devoting less than 20 years to an Epic Poem,' Coleridge wrote in a letter to his publisher, Joseph Cottle.

> Ten to collect materials and warm my mind with universal science. I would be a tolerable Mathematician, I would thoroughly know Mechanics, Hydrostatics, Optics, and

Astronomy, Botany, Metallurgy, Fossilism, Chemistry, Geology, Anatomy, Medicine – then the *mind of man* – then the *minds of men* – in all Travels, Voyages and Histories. So I would spend ten years – the next five to the composition of the poem – and the five last to the correction of it.

These Travels, Voyages and Histories would, of course, be important to 'Kubla Khan'.

On a summer evening in early June of 1797, while returning to Stowey from Bristol after delivering some poems to his publisher, Coleridge made a detour to visit a young north-country poet called William Wordsworth and his sister Dorothy who were living at Racedown, in Dorset. Although the two men had met briefly in August of 1795, and had been in correspondence and reading each other's work since that time, their friendship was not established until this memorable visit, which stretched on for weeks. Coleridge's enthusiasm for the Wordsworths was literally transporting, as he swept them along with him first to his own inadequate cottage, and then more permanently to a country mansion in Alfoxden, some four miles west of Stowey. Once safely ensconced within the same neighbourhood, the three friends embarked upon a kind of abbreviated pantisocratic existence, communing with Nature in the course of long walks, conversing and sharing their poetic interests. Both the letters of this period and Dorothy Wordsworth's delicate but incisive journal suggest that 'Nature' served as a kind of fourth companion during this summer idyll – certainly more of a real presence than was Sara Coleridge, whose domestic duties tended to keep her indoors at the Stowey cottage. The weather, the landscape, the different tones of the different hours of the day were reverently noted, discussed and described in exquisite detail by the threesome, and it is not difficult to imagine that this cultivated hypersensitivity to the natural world predisposed Coleridge to retain and savour in his prodigious memory particular images of Nature culled from his extensive reading.

Some time in early October, at the close of this happy summer of invigoration and inspiration, Coleridge took a long walk along the north Devon coast to Lynton, some twenty-four miles distant, this time alone and without the companionable conversation of his two friends. On the return trip, he was struck ill 'with a dysentry', as he later recorded in a footnote to the earliest manuscript account of this event (not to be confused with the later *published* account which prefaces the poem), and halfway home he turned aside to Ash Farm to spend the night. At least since the spring of 1796, Coleridge had fallen into the dangerous habit of taking opium, often for extended periods, in times of illness; now, at Ash Farm, as he later reported, he took two grains of opium to check the dysentery, and fell into the reverie in which he composed 'Kubla Khan'.

Ash Farm is, as Coleridge wrote in his manuscript account, 'between Porlock & Linton, a quarter of a mile from Culbone Church'. Porlock, village of ill-repute whence came the 'visitor on business' who interrupted Coleridge's transcription of his dream, is a tiny community of neat stone cottages and steep narrow streets, close to the sea. Its main hotel, the Ship Inn, is where Coleridge reputedly used to go to smoke; or so I was told by its manageress who, spotting me as yet another tourist on a Coleridge pilgrimage, took a perverse delight in attempting to puncture any illusions I may have wished to cherish about the poet:

'Of course, by the time he ended up here, he was potty with drugs, and as likely to be found rolling around in a ditch.'

Turning inland on the old toll road from Porlock, I met another, more genial, local historian in the person of the toll-keeper, an engaging elderly man who had himself walked through Coleridge's local paces. He had also taken opium, when hospitalised many years before, and still retained a vivid memory of the ensuing dream, in which he had seen himself sailing down along the most westerly Scottish Isles.

'I've never in my life seen them,' he said, 'but I *knew* that I was there. The man in the bed beside me was from Scotland and had told me about them.'

Past the toll, the road leisurely unfolded through forest which, on this defiantly brilliant day, presented itself less as a collection of trees than as a golden-green ethereal glow, an enveloping fairyland aether more than a mere prosaic forest.

Ash Farm is in a lonely position, far removed from other dwellings, and reached by a lengthy lane that runs narrowly through hedges. On this day of summer glory there could be nothing sinister about this isolation, but one could imagine how in bleaker weather, such as that in which Coleridge had most likely been forced to pay his visit, it would present a different aspect. Exmoor is, after all, *Lorna Doone* country, and the darker moods of its hills and moorlands are notoriously disquieting. An 'Esshe Farm' is listed in the 'Domesday Book', and indeed the snug, newly painted farmhouse gave the impression of being anciently established in the landscape. On the opposite side of the hedge, a sheep baaed at me, and blinked. For miles beyond, the grazed fields swelled and dipped.

At the house, I was greeted by an attractive woman with black hair and ivory skin, who did not look at all the country farmer's wife. To my joy, it was possible to get a room for the night in the old farmhouse, and the next morning I was pointed in the direction of Culbone Church, along a path that rolled down the steep slope of the farm's sheep-grazed field into a copse of forest nestled in the valley.

The roof of the little church is first seen from the height of a ravine within the forest, and scrambling down the sheer path I found it to be set delicately in its own long-grassed valley. It is the smallest complete parish church in England, and its walls date from at least the twelfth century. The evidence inside was that the church, with its handsome, bossed ceiling and intricately panelled pews, was still affectionately cared for, its minuscule congregation notwithstanding. Seen through the clear, diamond-patterned windows was the forest, and it would be a devoted worshipper indeed who could keep his attention inside the church on a day such as this, when the green leaves and blue sky were in such radiance. But the principal feature of Culbone Church is its raw setting. Reputedly, it stands on what was once a Celtic religious site; and even if this were not the informed opinion, one would surmise that this was anciently sacred ground. The forest slopes darkly and abruptly down the close-pressed valley walls that confine the little glen, manifesting a wild, primal beauty that is completely unrestrained by the grey delicacy of the little Christian icon. Indeed, there was something helpless and forlorn about the very existence of this evidence of a centuries' old attempt to civilise man's instinctive religious impulse. The little monument – so tiny because this was all the space the deep valley walls allowed it – only highlighted one's sense that tremendous, uncontainable forces permeated the woodland. Centuries ago, the parish woods had been inhabited by charcoal burners and a colony of lepers – a place holy, and in this weather, enchanted, but not unsuggestive of archaic savagery.

Departing from Culbone, my pilgrimage continued, in reverse, to Lynton, which towers over the ravines and East and West Lyn rivers from its cliff-top perch. Since the early eighteenth century it has attracted visitors, and the economy of it and Lynmouth, its seaside 'sister' village below, are today greatly dependent on tourists. The architecture of this spectacularly located town hardly suggests a summer resort, however, being heavy, oppressive, monumental and Victorian – more evocative of a prison or workhouse than of any place one might voluntarily go for recreation. And yet, unlike the dainty and inadequate church, these buildings seemed in some weird way to echo the land's own force, which is darkly sombre here, even on a soft July evening in golden dying light. Beside the village, the West Lyn comes pouring down from the cliffs into the boulder-beached sea. There are a number of trails mapped out for visitors that parallel the region's more picturesque streams and cascades, but in Coleridge's day these would have been left to one's own discovery.

West of Lynton lies some of the most dramatic coastal scenery in England. A perilous cliff-line, swept to its edge by moorlands, over-looks the foreboding Valley of the Rocks, which sprawls and spills into the sea. Strangely, the sea on this blue day seemed flat and dull, an impression that was perhaps exaggerated by its contrast to the marked energy of the convoluted rubble of boulders for which the valley is named – naked manifestations of the earth's latent forces. Without question, if Professor Lowes had never written his acclaimed book, one would turn here, to the scenery of Exmoor – the scenery, after all, last experienced by Coleridge before his reverie at Ash Farm – for the inspiration of Xanadu. Even the tourist brochure (which, by the way, makes no mention of Coleridge) written to guide the visitor around the charms of Lynton inevitably falls into language worthy of 'Kubla Khan': 'The wild and fantastic heights, making for precipitous hills, valleys and gentle streams, combine to make the whole area a paradise ... while the romance of the place makes it a number-one place for honeymooners.' Or, more aptly, for women wailing for demon lovers (as a footnote, it is worth mentioning that the essayist and critic William Hazlitt, in a reminiscence of making this walk from Stowey to Lynton in Coleridge's company some eight months after his reverie at Ash Farm, recalls the 'screaming flight' of the gulls in the Valley of the Rocks – perhaps the inspiration for a woman wailing in a savage, romantic chasm).

Coleridge himself gave various dates for the composition of 'Kubla Khan'. In the Crewe Manuscript he cites 'the fall of the year, 1797'; in the published preface it is 'the summer of 1797'. In his Notebook of 1810, he recalls the spring of 1798, while in 'retirement between Linton & Porlock', as the first occasion on which he had 'recourse to Opium', a statement which is manifestly false, unless, as his biographer Richard Holmes suggests, by 'recourse' Coleridge meant his first use of the drug 'for non-medicinal purposes'. Scholars today tend to support the October 1797 date as being most probable, although Lowes' preferential date was the summer of 1798. In either case, there is no reason to doubt the essential inspirational sources for the poem – the travel books cited in the Notebooks and the wild Exmoor landscape.

Between the date of composition and the poem's actual publication in 1816, there are strikingly few references, by Coleridge or others, to this most famous of poems. The earliest is found in Dorothy Wordsworth's Journal for October 1798, when she and her brother were with Coleridge in Germany. This historic first mention is hardly illustrious, being based on a bad pun: she speaks of carrying '*Kubla* to a fountain', i.e. a *Khan*, or watering 'can' (evidently, Coleridge's pronunciation of the word rhymed with 'ran'). Sara Coleridge refers to the poem in a letter as *Koula Khan*.

More compelling is the description left by Sir Thomas Talfourd, of Coleridge's recitation of the poem, before its publication, at one of Charles Lamb's famous Wednesday night parties. In Talfourd's account, Coleridge appears to have almost subsumed the role of the inspired, visionary bard of his own final stanza:

There [at Lamb's] Coleridge sometimes, though rarely, took his seat; and then the genial hubbub of voices was still: critics, philosophers, and poets, were contented to listen; and toil-worn lawyers, clerks from the India House, and members of the Stock Exchange, grew romantic while he spoke ... Although he looked much older than he was, his hair being silvered all over, and his person tending to corpulency, there was about him no trace of bodily sickness or mental decay, but rather an air of voluptuous repose. His benignity of manner placed his auditors entirely at their ease, and inclined them to listen to the sweet, low tone in which he began to discourse on some high theme. Whether he had won for his greedy listener only some raw lad, or charmed a circle of beauty, rank, and wit, who hung breathless on his words, he talked with equal eloquence; for his subject, not his audience, inspired him. At first his tones were conversational; he seemed to dally with the shadows of the subject and with fantastic images which bordered it; but gradually the thought grew deeper, and the voice deepened with the thought; the stream gathering strength, seemed to bear along with it all things which opposed its progress, and blended them with its current; and stretching away among regions tinted with ethereal colours, was lost at airy distance in the horizon of the fancy ... Coleridge was sometimes induced to recite portions of 'Christabel', then enshrined in manuscript from eyes profane, and gave a bewitching effect to its wizard lines. But more peculiar in its beauty than this, was his recitation of Kubla Khan. As he repeated the passage –

> A damsel with a dulcimer
> In a vision once I saw:
> It was an Abyssinian maid,
> And on her dulcimer she played,
> Singing of Mount Abora!

his voice seemed to mount, and melt into air, as the images grew
more visionary, and the suggested associations more remote.

The year 1797, which has been fairly called Coleridge's *annus
mirabilis*, also saw the composition of *The Ancient Mariner*, and the
first part of 'Christabel', as well as 'This Lime-Tree Bower My Prison', one of his most successful 'conversational' poems. In 1798,
Coleridge and Wordsworth jointly published *Lyrical Ballads*, a landmark of Romantic literature, and of English poetry in general.
Although Coleridge's role was later short-changed in this venture,
the original inspiration had been for the two poets to divide the
poetical province, with Wordsworth taking commonplace subjects
and Coleridge the supernatural.

Shortly after the publication of *Lyrical Ballads*, in the same year,
Coleridge, initially accompanied by the Wordsworths, departed
from Nether Stowey for Germany, intent on learning German and
philosophy, which 'philosophising' was to shape to a great extent
his subsequent views on metaphysics and religion. He remained
abroad some ten months, and on returning, he brought his family to
Keswick in the Lake District, not far from where the Wordsworths
had settled.

Coleridge's health had by this time broken down, his most serious
afflictions being rheumatic fever and opium addiction. Although
expansive on the topic of most of his ailments, he refused for a long
while to acknowledge his drug addiction, maintaining, to himself as
well as others, that his use was only medicinal. He now made other
excursions abroad, to Malta and Italy, principally in quest of better
health and spirits – a quest that would consume the rest of his life. On
his return to England in 1807, he at last separated from his long-
suffering wife.

Henceforth, his time was for the most part spent in giving lectures
and writing – or planning to write – the sporadic periodical he had
founded to treat 'Principles of Political Justice, of Morality, and of
Taste,' entitled *The Friend*. The year 1810 saw a breach in his long
friendship with Wordsworth, the cause of which was a criticism of
Coleridge made by Wordsworth in confidence to a mutual friend,

who irresponsibly passed it on, according to Coleridge, in the following form: 'Wordsworth has commissioned me to tell you that he has no hope of you, that you have been a rotten drunkard and rotted out your entrails by intemperance, and have been an absolute nuisance in his family.' Undoubtedly, as Wordsworth subsequently took elaborate pains to state, a well-intentioned observation had been severely garbled, but the incident does none the less highlight certain truths about Coleridge's condition. In order to counteract the depression that followed his opium bouts, he had resorted to the 'stimulus' of alcohol. In the same year, the ever-loyal Dorothy Wordsworth had written to a friend that Coleridge 'lies in bed, always till after 12 o'clock, sometimes much later ... He never leaves his own parlour except at dinner or tea and sometimes supper, and then he always seems impatient to get back to his solitude – he goes the moment his food is swallowed. Sometimes he does not speak a word.'

At last, in 1816, Coleridge made a brave move, and acknowledging the extent of his drug addiction, placed himself under the care of a doctor in Highgate, then a village north of London.

'... for the first week I shall not, *I must not be permitted* to leave your House,' Coleridge wrote to Dr Gillman, prior to his admittance to his charge. '... Delicately or indelicately, this *must* be done: and both the Servant and the young Man must receive absolute commands from you on no account to fetch any thing for me. The stimulus of Conversation suspends the terror that haunts my mind; but when I am alone, the horrors, I have suffered from Laudanum, the degradation, the blighted Utility, almost overwhelm me.'

Although intending to remain in Highgate for only a month, his sojourn there lasted for eighteen years, or until the end of his life. It was in the summer of 1816 that two of his poetic masterpieces – 'Kubla Khan' and 'Christabel' – were finally brought to publication, along with the lesser 'Pains of Sleep'. This latter poem, it has been suggested, depicts the flip side of an opium high – the junkie's night terrors. As noted earlier, the published version of 'Kubla Khan' differed in subtle but often important respects from that of an earlier manuscript, a fact that suggests that the original 'dream-poem' received revisions over the years in the course of its recitations. Some scholars believe that the concluding stanza, differing in subject, metrics and mood from the rest of the poem, was the most revised, if not an altogether later addition. A yet more extreme view is that the poem was a self-consciously crafted conventional work that received its romantic preface from Coleridge as an excuse for its incompleteness. But most would feel, as Lowes says, that 'nobody in his waking senses could have fabricated [the] magical [final] eighteen lines'.

The poem was by no means received with universal acclaim on its publication. Hazlitt lambasted it in the *Edinburgh Review*, pouncing on Coleridge's self-effacing statement in his introduction that as far as his own opinions were concerned, he was publishing the poem 'rather as a psychological curiosity, than on the ground of any *poetic* merits'.

'In these opinions of the candid author,' Hazlitt wrote, 'we entirely concur', and he goes on to add that the lines 'smell strongly' of the anodyne of laudanum and, citing the sedative powers of the anodyne, suggests that 'a dozen or so lines . . . would reduce the most irritable of critics to a state of inaction'. On the other hand, 'Kubla Khan' had its strong champions, perhaps most notably Lord Byron, at whose request, according to Coleridge, this most Byronic of poetic works was published.

A few of the scattered images of the fragmentary poem turned up, some two years after its composition at Ash Farm, in a trivial work, first published in the *Morning Post*, entitled 'Lines Composed in a Concert-Room':

> Dear Maid! whose form in solitude I seek,
> Such songs in such a mood to hear thee sing,
> It were a deep delight! . . .

And in his rambling prose essay in defence of Trinitarian Christianity, entitled *Aids to Reflection* and published in 1825, the familiar imagery of fountains, 'odorous and flowering thickets' opening into 'spots of greenery', grottoes and caves is worked into a rather confusing 'allegory of the Mystic' – the same allegory, incidentally, that was referred to in the previous chapter in connection with James Bruce. But apart from these weak reverberations, 'Kubla Khan' left no impression on Coleridge's own later works. His summer day of poetic inspiration was in any case short-lived, his last poem of any note, the blank verse 'To William Wordsworth', being composed in 1806. Coleridge's literary critical masterwork *Biographia Literaria*, published in 1817, was his last important literary work of any kind.

In 1833, the breach with Wordsworth was patched up, and Coleridge returned with his old friend for a tour of Germany and the Low Countries. And in September of the following year, he died at Highgate. An autopsy revealed an abnormally large heart, exacerbated by early rheumatic fever, and a massive cyst in the right side of his chest, between which his lungs had been compressed. Coleridge's sufferings, about which many friends had grown sceptical, had, then, been real enough, and his characteristic and maligned 'indolence' as well as opium use, therefore, somewhat vindicated.

One of the dangers of some critical treatment – as, indeed, of this one – is that they can be taken to imply that the 'phenomenon' of 'Kubla Khan' was the inevitable result of a combination of opium and eclectic reading – that drug plus travel literature equals masterpiece. But whatever the stimulants, the creative 'process' took place within the uniquely teeming, fertile, dreaming mind of Samuel Taylor Coleridge. That this armchair Odysseus had ranged over so many interior landscapes, 'seeing the towns and learning the minds of men', was itself an expression of his most characteristic passion to know all things of the world, to journey to the furthest horizons of intellect and imagination. He was, as Wordsworth is reputed to have said, his voice breaking, 'The most *wonderful* man I have ever known.'

In a postscript chapter to his exemplary biography of Coleridge, Richard Holmes poses the interesting question of how Coleridge would have been perceived by posterity if he had died in the course of his Mediterranean 'exile' in Malta and Italy – as indeed his friends half expected he would – and posits that 'he would be seen as part of that meteoric, Romantic tradition of young writers, like Keats, Shelley, or Byron … who lived and died in a blaze of premature talents'. Coleridge was, one must remind oneself, only twenty-five years old in 1797, his *annus mirabilis*. 'Kubla Khan', Holmes suggests, unpublished at this date, might have existed only as an 'oral memory, uncommitted to manuscript, a true piece of Romantic folklore'. As it is, Coleridge's poetic output is seen within the context of a relatively long life of ill-conceived and half-finished projects, and he himself as possessed of a genius that, like his famous poem, was filled with scattered images, fragmented and incomplete. One cannot help wondering whether in later years, when paralysed by doubt and an inability to actualise his many projected schemes, Coleridge looked back with longing on that day when his poetic powers had unfolded with such miraculous lack of effort. Significantly, there is in 'Kubla Khan' itself a manifestation of the fear of creative impotence which would torment Coleridge throughout his life: the conditionals 'could' and 'would' of the Mystic/poet's desire to revive symphony and song in this case speak legions. Thus while 'Kubla Khan' represents Coleridge's summer kingdom of enchantment, its dome of pleasure is already overshadowed by a dark foreboding.

Where, one also has to wonder, would the 'lost' one hundred and fifty or so lines have taken the poem? Coleridge addressed the poem's incompleteness at the conclusion of its published preface: '... from the still surviving recollections in his mind, the author has frequently purposed to finish for himself what had been originally, as it were, given to him. *Aurion adion asô,*' Coleridge wrote, paraphrasing Theocritus ('Tomorrow I shall sing a sweeter song') 'but the tomorrow is yet to come.'

Coleridge and the companions of his romantic walks could not have guessed at the changes that have been wrought in the world since the 'glad morning' of their youth. And whether it is the world that has most changed, or our perceptions of it, we do know this: that it is unlikely that, ever again, a Xanadu will be yielded from contemporary descriptions. We know now that the tomorrow will never come.

I had imagined that on completing my journeys I would return to 'Kubla Khan' with a heightened poetic vision – indeed, with something approximating the vividness of the original opium dream; and it is, perhaps, a testimony to Coleridge's transcendent genius that I did not. As the opening lines unfold, the same images rise in front of me as before – a place dark and craggy, with perhaps more of Florida's shaggy greenery than of anything else, but essentially reminiscent of nowhere I have seen.

But ironically, I was, after all, left with an enduring and unexpected memory of Xanadu. It harbours few images at all; just the bare bones of Shangdu's ruined vanished city, with light and geese above and somewhere down below the outshine of a limitless plain of golden grass – nothing more to fill that magnificent, plundered void, that wasteland of a palace, those fallen walls and towers.

HELPFUL
SOURCES

Helpful Sources

COLERIDGE

Chambers, E.K., *Samuel Taylor Coleridge: A Biographical Study*, Oxford, 1938.

Coburn, Kathleen (ed.), *The Notebooks of Samuel Taylor Coleridge* (especially volume 1, 1794–1804), New York, 1957.

Coleridge, Samuel Taylor, *The Complete Poetical Works of Samuel Taylor Coleridge*, edited by Ernest Hartley Coleridge, Oxford, 1912.

——*The Complete Works of Samuel Taylor Coleridge*, edited by W.G.T. Shedd, New York, 1884. (*Aids to Reflection*, the essay referred to in the last two chapters, comprises volume 1 of this 7-volume collection.)

Griggs, Earl Leslie (ed.), *Collected Letters of Samuel Taylor Coleridge*, Oxford, 1956.

Holmes, Richard, *Coleridge: Early Visions*, London, 1989.

Lefebure, Molly, *Samuel Taylor Coleridge: A Bondage of Opium*, New York, 1974.

Lowes, John Livingston, *The Road to Xanadu*, Boston and New York, 1927. (Much quoted in, and essential to, my book.)

Noyes, Russell (ed.), *English Romantic Poetry and Prose*, New York, 1956. (A good basic anthology of Romantic literature, and handy for giving an introduction to Coleridge through the eyes of his contemporaries. Full references to contemporary writers are found in the bibliographies of Holmes and Chambers.)

Suther, Marshall, *Visions of Xanadu*, New York, 1965. (Anti-Lowes: echoes of 'Kubla Khan' culled from Coleridge's own writing, thus indicating a predilection for Xanadu-esque imagery. Provocative, but far-fetched.)

INNER MONGOLIA

Boyle, John Andrew, 'The Seasonal Residences of the Great Khan Ögödei', *Central Asiatic Journal*, 16 (1972): 125–31.

Bushell, S.W., 'Notes on a Journey outside the Great Wall of China', *Proceedings of the Royal Geographical Society*, 18, no. 2 (1874): 149–168. Also see 'Notes on the old Mongolian Capital of Shangtu' in *Journal of the Royal Asiatic Society*, 7 (1875): 329–38. Also in *Journal of the Royal Geographical Society*, 44 (1874): 73–97.

Campbell, C.W., 'A Journey in Mongolia', *Great Britain Foreign Office Report, China*, vol. 1 (1904): 11–12.

Cleaves, Francis Woodman, 'The "Fifteen 'Palace Poems'" by K'o Chiu-ssu', *Harvard Journal of Asiatic Studies*, 20 (1957): 391–479.

Dalrymple, William, *In Xanadu: A Quest*, London, 1989.

Gerbillon, John François, 'Voyage dans la Tartarie Occidentale, par l'ordre de l'empereur de la Chine ou à sa suite, en 1688 & 1698', in *Histoire générale des voyages ...*, edited by Antoine François Prévost, vol. 9, p. 469, vol. 10, p. 70, La Haye, 1747–80. Also published as 'Travels into Western Tartary, by Order of the Emperor of China, or in his retinue, between the Years 1688, and 1698', in *A New General Collection of Voyages and Travels*, edited by John Green (the Astley Collection), vol. iv, London, 1747.

Harada, Yoshito (ed.), *Shang-tu: The Summer Capital of the Yüan Dynasty* (mostly in Japanese), Tokyo, 1941.

Impey, Lawrence, 'Shangtu, The Summer Capital of Kublai Khan', *Geographical Review*, 15 (1925): 584–604.

Morgan, David, *The Mongols*, Oxford, 1986.

Polo, Marco, *The Travels*, translated by Ronald Latham (Penguin Classics), London, 1958.

Pozdneev, A., *Mongolia e Mongolij*, St Petersburg, 1898. (Quoted passages were translated from the Russian by Gina Kovarski.)

Rashid al-Din, *The Successors of Genghis Khan*, translated from the Persian by J.A. Boyle, New York, 1971.

Rossabi, Morris, *Khubilai Khan: His Life and Times*, Berkeley, 1988. (Dr Rossabi's more recent work *Voyager from Xanadu* (New York 1992) is an intriguing counterpart to the accounts of journeys made to Xanadu – written by an envoy of Khubilai Khan, it describes the journey of the first person from China to visit Europe.

Steinhardt, Nancy Shatzman, *Chinese Imperial City Planning*, Honolulu,

1990. (Professor Steinhardt is the principal source for Mongolian imperial architecture for this book. In particular, she is to be credited for the suggestion that Shangdu was used by the khans for recreation and hunting after 1262, the foundation date for Da-du.)

'Imperial Architecture Along the Mongolian Road to Dadu', *Ars Orientalis*, 18 (1988): 59–93.

'The Plan of Khubilai Khan's Imperial City', *Artibus Asiae*, 44 (1983): 137–158.

A great deal of poetry was written during the Yuan dynasty by Chinese envoys and officials in the Khan's court describing their visits to, and impressions of, Shangdu, or the Upper capital. Poems quoted in the first chapter are to be found in the following works:

Liu Guan (1270–1342), exerpts from the *Shangjing jixing shi* (A Poetic Diary of the Upper Capital), Beijing: Gugong bowuyuan (Palace Museum), 1930 (a photolithographic reprint of the early fifteenth-century woodblock), 6a–7a.

Yuan Jue (1262–1327), 'Miscellaneous Songs on the Upper Capital', in the *Qingrong jushi ji* (Collected Literary Works of the Lay Buddhist Who Keeps His Form Pure), *Sibu beiyao* ed., 15: 5a–6a.

Zhou Boqi (d. *c*.1367), exerpts from the *Bowen jinguang ji* (Collected Poems by Bowne [Zhou Boqi] Composed in Proximity to the Light [of the Emperor]), in the *Yuan shixuan, chuji*, Taipei: Shijie shuju (1962 reprint of the 1751 edn), pp.857–1865.

The poems are so evocative that I regret not having been able to place them all in my work. Most of the poems have never been translated. All English translations appearing here were made by Dr Richard John Lynn, who, as a result of this 'assignment', is working on a forthcoming collection of poems about Shangdu translated into English.

FLORIDA

Adicks, Richard (ed.), *Le Conte's Report on East Florida*, Orlando, 1978.

Bartram, William, *Travels Through North & South Carolina, Georgia, East & West Florida, the Cherokee Country, the Extensive Territories of the*

Muscogulges, or Creek Confederacy, and the Country of the Chactaws, Philadelphia, 1791. (Reprint by Penguin Nature Library, New York, 1988.)

Cabell, James, *The St Johns River: a parade of diversities*, New York, 1943.

Essoe, Gabe, *Tarzan of the Movies*, New York, 1968.

Glunt, James and Ulrich Phillips (eds.), *Florida Plantation Records, From the Papers of George Noble James*, St Louis, 1927.

Hodges, Frederick W., *Spanish Explorers in the Southern States*, New York, 1907.

Motte, Jacob Rhett, *Journey into Wilderness; account of an army surgeon's life in camp and field during the Creek and Seminole Wars, 1836–1838*, edited by James F. Sunderman, Gainesville, 1953.

Muir, John, *A Thousand-Mile Walk To the Gulf*, New York, 1916.

Olschki, Leonardo, 'Ponce de León's Fountain of Youth', *The Hispanic American Review*, xxi, no. 3 (1941): 361–385. (In a striking coincidence, the two principal poetic strands that apparently combined to shape this legend were the *Letter of Prester John* and the *Roman d'Alexandre*, two medieval works that refer to India and Ethiopia – the two other places that inspired the imagery of Xanadu.)

Ribaut, Jean, *The Whole & True Discovereye of Terra Florida* (facsimile reprint of London edition of 1563), De Land, Florida, 1927.

State of Florida, Geological Survey, *The Springs of Florida*, Tallahassee, 1977.

Tebeau, Charlton W., *A History of Florida*, Coral Gables, Florida, 1971.

Whitman, Alice, 'Transportation in Territorial Florida', *Florida Historical Quarterly*, xvii (July 1938): 25–53.

KASHMIR

Ahmad, S.M. and R.Bano, *Historical Geography of Kashmir*, New Delhi, 1984. (A catalogue of ancient references to important sites.)

Anonymous, *Phallic Miscellanies; Facts and Phases of Ancient and Modern Sex Worship, as Illustrated Chiefly in the Religions of India*, London (?), 1891. (A curiosity, and chiefly valuable for its description of early rites of lingam worship.)

Bamzai, Prithivi Nath Kaul, *A History of Kashmir: Political, Social, Cultural, From the Earliest Times to the Present Day*, rev. edn, Delhi, 1973.

Bernier, François, *Histoire de la dernière révolution des états du Grand Mogol*, Paris, 1670–71. Also published as *Travels in the Mogul Empire, A.D. 1656–1668*, translated by Irving Brock, edited by Archibald Constable, 2nd rev. edn, London, 1914.

Beveridge, Henry, *The Túzuk-i-Jahángírí* (Jahangir's autobiography), translated by Alexander Rogers, London, 1909 and 1914.

Crowe, Sylvia, Sheila Haywood, Susan Jellicoe and Gordon Patterson, *The Gardens of Mughul India*, London, 1972. (A work of scholarship and love; sheer pleasure.)

Hassnain, F. M., Y. Miura and V. Pandita, *Sri Amarnatha Cave*, New Delhi, 1987. (A pilgrim's 'manual' to making this holy journey.)

Lamb, Alistair, *Kashmir: A Disputed Legacy, 1846–1990*, Hertingfordbury, Hertfordshire, 1991.

Lawrence, Walter R., *The Valley of Kashmir*, London, 1895. (A comprehensive description of the valley, including its geology and flora, and the political and social history of its inhabitants.)

Maurice, Revd Thomas, *The History of Hindostan; its Arts, and its Sciences, as Connected with the History of the Other Great Empires of Asia, During the Most Ancient Periods of the World*, London, 1795.

Morgan, Kenneth W. (ed.), *The Religion of the Hindus*, New York, 1953. (An informative and readable treatment of a complex subject – I was also helped by the more concise discussion and bibliography of the *Encyclopaedia Britannica*'s chapter on Hinduism.

Pandit, Ranjit Sitaram (trans. and ed.), *Rájatainangini: The Saga of the Kings of Kasmír*, New Delhi, 1968.

Rennell, James, *Memoir of a Map of Hindoostan; or the Mogul's Empire*, London, 3rd edn, 1793. (Reprinted by Editions Indian, Calcutta, 1976.)

Zaehner, R. C., *Hinduism*, 2nd edn, Oxford, 1966. (Scholarly, and systematic. A good source of reference, but a somewhat heavy-going cover-to-cover read.)

ETHIOPIA

Alvarez, Francis, 'The Prester John of the Indies: A True Relation of the Lands of Prester John, being the Narrative of the Portuguese Embassy to Ethiopia in 1520 written by Father Francisco Alvarez', in *Hakluytus Postumus, or Purchas His Pilgrimes*, vol. 7, Glasgow, 1905.

Budge, Sir E.A. Wallis, *A History of Ethiopia, Nubia and Abyssinia*, London, 1928.

Bruce, James, *Travels to Discover the Sources of the Nile in the years 1768, 1769, 1770, 1771, 1772 and 1773*, Edinburgh, 1790. (A complete edition, outside of a special collection, is both hard to find and a momentous undertaking. A good excerpted edition is that selected and edited by C.F. Beckingham, Edinburgh, 1969.)

Cheesman, R.E., *Lake Tana and the Blue Nile: An Abyssinian Quest*, London, 1936. (An account of the first successful attempt to chart systematically the Blue Nile course.)

Greenfield, Richard, *Ethiopia: a New Political History*, New York, 1965. (Focuses on twentieth-century Ethiopian history, and particularly Haile Selassie's reign up until the coup attempt and its aftermath in the early 1960s.)

Lobo, Father Jeronymo, *A Voyage to Abyssinia. By Father Jerome Lobo*, translated from the French by Samuel Johnson, London, 1735. (Also included in this volume is a translation of Father Paez's earlier description of the Nile fountains, from which Lobo's account is almost certainly derived.)

Moorehead, Alan, *The Blue Nile*, London, 1962. (The great river, from start to finish.)

Purchas, Samuel (ed.), 'Africa. The Seventh Booke. Relations of Ethiopian rarities, collected out of Frier Luys a Spanish Author', in *Purchas His Pilgrimage*, London, 1617. (See especially page 843ff, 'Of the Hill Amara'.)

Reid, J.M., *Traveller Extraordinary: The Life of James Bruce of Kinnaird*, New York, 1968.

Taddesse Tamrat, 'Ethiopia, the Red Sea and the Horn', in *The Cambridge History of Africa*, edited by Roland Oliver, vol. 3, Cambridge, 1977. (Includes an account of the institution and fall of Mount Amara.)

Thesiger, Wilfred, *The Life of My Choice*, London, 1987. (Includes, amid much else, an account of Thesiger's boyhood in Haile Selassie's Ethiopia and travels in the country's wildest reaches. A portrait of Abyssinia as it was and will never be again, by the last great traveller of our age).